Hydroponics for Beginners

Ultimate guide 2021

Contents

PEST CONTROL

CHAPTER 7

AVOID MYTHS AND ERRORS

LAST WORDS

INTRODUCTION

When we think of gardening, we often see in our heads a man or a woman with four legs crouching on the field of the earth. They dig a hole, put it in seeds, and even close it in all the plants they buy, and it's done. Or maybe we think of gardening compatible with agriculture and imagine the same thing; except that this times no one is crouching, but a series of mechanical inventions that do so much work for them. We certainly do not think of interior design, because it is more compatible with hanging plants and decorative greens than with the concept of gardening. This would indicate that our main characteristic that separates gardening from several plants is the dirt itself, the soil that is part of Mother Earth. But the facts are very different.

There are many types of gardening. A classic flower bed in the backyard is just one of them. Here we look at another: hydroponics. The claim that hydroponics is a new fashion in the gardening world will discredit its history regarding the hanging gardens of Babylon and the floating gardens of the Aztecs. There are even Egyptian hieroglyphs that describe the hydroponic form. Recently, hydroponics has also gained a place in NASA's space program. Of course, this is not a new fashion. Commercial breeders and scientists are approaching this method, which results in more hydroponic setups and further research on the benefits of hydroponics.

How does hydroponics differ from traditional gardening? As the name suggests (water), water plays a vital role. The hydroponic garden does not use any land. Instead, hydroponic gardens use nutrient-based solutions during the water cycle. The hydroponic garden throws away the soil and instead uses an inert growing medium such as clay granules, vermiculite, perlite, or one of the many others that will appear in this book. This allows the roots of the plant to touch the nutrient solution directly, to get more oxygen because they are not buried in the soil and together support growth.

The growth it promotes can be incredible. When properly managed, a hydroponic environment can ripen plants up to 25% faster than typical soil gardens.

Also, plants that grow 25% faster can produce up to 30% more! This is because plants do not have to work as hard to maintain nutrients in a hydroponic configuration as in a more traditional arrangement. Because the roots get everything they need to provide the plants with nutrients, the plant can focus on growing the top instead of growing the roots for conservation.

However, using a hydroponic package offers even more benefits than just targeted plant development. Although the name Hydro is well known, hydroponic gardens use less water than traditional earth gardens. This is because the hydroponic system is a closed system. This means that there is less runoff from the soil, evaporation or wastewater in the hydroponic system. Therefore, a hydroponic garden, if properly configured and maintained, will produce larger plants faster and with less impact on the environment. Everything seems to benefit everyone.

However, hydroponic gardens have slight drawbacks compared to traditional earth gardens. The biggest and most evident of these drawbacks is that creating a hydroponic garden, whatever its size, costs more than a vegetable garden. In a rock garden, it is enough to dig a hole, to plant a plant or seeds than to water it from time to time. That doesn't mean you have a healthy, well-functioning garden, but it's easy to start with. A hydroponic garden costs time and money, especially if you've never installed it. If you do not maintain the hydroponic setup, it is unlikely that these plants remain alive. Maintenance is very important here, that's why the whole chapter is devoted to this subject. There are many types of hydroponic gardens that we can set up, and some of them are riskier than others. For example, a pump-based configuration (such as a drain and flow system) can cause the pump to clog if not correctly maintained, and the clogged pump can see all dead plants as a result.

It should be noted that we focus on hydroponics, which despite the similarity of the name, is not identical to gardening in water. Aquaponic gardening is actually a mixture of hydroponics and fish farming. Basically, Aquaponics is a hydroponic garden in which fish are introduced into the system. These fish produce waste products in the water that provide plants with nutrients. In return, the vegetables from the aquaponics garden clean the water for the fish. In this way, the aquaponic garden offers both farmed fish and farm plants. Aquaponics gardening is a great way to grow and grow food for sustainable development. However, aquaponic gardening is beyond the scope of this book.

In this book, we will first examine the different types of hydroponic gardens that we can create. These will be systems, from drains to drains and currents, from aeroponics to humidity management systems. We will take a look at the pros and cons they offer so that you have the knowledge to choose the type of system that works best for you. Next, we look at how these systems are structured. Although we are not going to build an existing system, we will examine the necessary equipment and examine the specifics of the most popular styles.

After building our systems, we will talk about the cycle of hydroponic gardens. This means that we will examine how we configure our crops and plant seeds and discuss various issues related to the lighting and pruning of our plants. Once we understand how to operate these systems, we will spend some time exploring the different systems best suited for hydroponics. We also highlighted nutrition to find out what exactly we mean when we use the word and what nutrients we deliver to our systems.

If we understand the functioning and nutrition of our hydroponic gardens, we can start a discussion on nature conservation. This is one of the key areas that we need to understand if we are to succeed in our hydroponic gardens.

Without proper maintenance, we cannot expect adequate growth if we tackle congestion and poor ph. We will move from maintenance to pests which themselves require a different form of maintenance. Fortunately, pests do are not as common in the configuration hydroponics as in traditional gardens. Finally, we will examine the errors and myths that often arise when creating and maintaining a hydroponic garden.

Although creating gardens takes more time than traditional gardens, the knowledge in this book will help you create your own. But the benefits of hydroponics speak for themselves: larger plants in less time. Who wouldn't want that?

Advantages and disadvantages

Each product growth system has advantages and disadvantages. It is good to know what it is before starting the DIY system. We will first look at the benefits.

Benefits

It grows everywhere

There are large areas of the world that cannot be used for growing food, especially desserts and arid areas. However, as long as you can bring water to these places, you can set up a hydroponic system and grow plants.

Since a large part of the dessert, the room is classified as "useless," this is a real bonus!

Fewer pests

Soil pests often infect plants. As the soil is not an essential element of the hydroponic system, the risk of disease is reduced. It should be noted that this will not be eliminated as airborne pests can still introduce diseases into your hydroponic system.

Greenhouses or indoor crops act as a barrier against pests. One of the advantages of a greenhouse is that you can release useful insects that eat the parasites. If you are using a greenhouse, these useful insects are included.

Faster growth time

Plants were grown in hydroponics grow faster because they have access to all nutrients and trace elements. They offer greater efficiency and are more resistant to parasites. In short, hydroponic cultivation gives better results than traditional cultivation methods.

Research shows that lettuce grown in hydroponics can produce up to 41 kilograms / square meter per year. Unlike just three and a half pounds / ten square feet (three points, nine kilograms / square meter) per year when grown conventionally.

Water consumption in hydroponics was ten times lower than that of soil. The hydroponic harvest was 11 times higher than in the ground.

These figures seem to speak for themselves, but additional costs must be borne for hydroponics which must be taken into account. In this study, they also calculated that energy costs in hydroponics were 82 times higher than in soil. It is very important to know the business operations.

Better control

With hydroponic farming, you can monitor and adjust the nutrients in the water. This allows much greater control of the growing environment and provides the best possible performance in the shortest possible time.

Water consumption

Research shows that hydroponics uses nine to ten percent less water than conventional crops desired in a field. This is because the water mainly flows through; the water is only lost by evaporation or exchange of water.

Cons

Thanks to the advantages, you always have disadvantages.
Let us look at them further.

High configuration costs

Hydroponics has higher upfront costs than plants that grow in the ground. Indeed, you need certain elements to start:

- Water reservoir
- The water circulation pump
- Plant growth kit (NFT, DWC)
- Growth medium
- Need to buy nutrients
- Sometimes artificial light sources

Airborne diseases

Although the risk of soil-borne diseases is lower, airborne diseases can occur and, due to the nature of hydroponics, these diseases can spread quickly between plants when planted closer to each other. other.

It is important to know the main symptoms of plant diseases and to react as quickly as possible.

Another example of a disease that is not in the air is pythium (root rot), which can get into the hydroponic system through water and cause the roots to brown. Fortunately, you can control most of them via the appropriate system design that we will discuss later in this book.

Knowledge, skills

It is relatively easy to understand the principles underlying hydroponics, although some experience is required. However, to properly start the system, you need to know the different devices involved and how to monitor and regulate the nutrient content.

Getting it right is necessary to create a sustainable system, but it can be a steep learning curve. If you do not succeed the first time, you see it as a learning experience, not a failure.

Oversight

If you are growing plants using conventional soil-based methods, you can let the plants sit for a few days. Nature is used to finding a way for plants to grow in almost any situation.

Once you have created a hydroponic system, you should often look for visible issues and nutritional values.

A mechanical error can have a very negative effect on the hydroponic system and possibly kill plants!

Of course, there are many ways to automate parts of the system, but that shouldn't be your main concern when creating your first entertainment system.

Current

Electricity is needed to run the pumps, provide artificial light, heat or cooling and airflow. All of these extras result in a higher electricity bill, which incurs additional costs.

Water and electricity generally do not mix well, which poses a safety risk.

If something happens to food, systems can suffer surprisingly quickly. You should have the backup option to run the pump on a commercial system for several hours. This can be done with a solar system or an emergency generator.

Hydroponics vs. Aquaponics

You may have heard of aquaponics as an alternative to hydroponics. It works on similar principles, but it is not the same thing.

In hydroponics, plants grow in water enriched with the right nutrients to stimulate growth. These nutrients should be added regularly. This is why it is so essential to check pH, nutrient content, and temperature regularly. This is the only way to be sure of having the optimal environment for plant growth.

Partial water exchange is often necessary for hydroponics. Then you need to make sure that the pH and nutrient levels have returned to the recommended level. The aquaponics system is mainly a closed cycle with minimal water loss.

The critical difference between the two systems is that in aquaponics, there are fish in the water. You need to feed fish that convert protein-rich foods into ammonia. Bacteria transform ammonia into nitrates, which are plant foods.

Fish provide 10 of the 13 nutrients a plant needs. Water always returns to the aquarium. This makes hydroponics more autonomous than desired but needs more knowledge, which makes the hydroponic system more complicated there.

You must supplement the aquaponic system with three nutrients: iron, potassium, and calcium. The rest comes from fish and fish feed.

It is also important to know that the aquaponics system must be recycled before growing plants. This guarantees the presence of bacteria that convert the fish waste into plant nutrients. This means that growing plants with the aquaponic system takes longer than with the hydroponic system.

Installing Aquaponic systems is also more expensive.

For these reasons, hydroponics has become a more popular option in commercial farming, while aquaponics is the preferred option for small-scale production, backyard systems or university demonstration systems.

Of course, many people prefer one of these systems, because both offer better performance, faster harvests, and less space than soil-based farming methods.

If you want to read a good book on aquaponics, I recommend you read Nick Brooke's book, *Aquaponics for Beginners*.

In the next chapter, we will begin our hydroponic journey by examining what equipment we need to get started.

Equipment

Surveillance equipment

PH meter

PH is a measure of the acidity or alkalinity of water. PH 7 is indifferent. PH values from 1 to 6 are acidic, and values from 8 to 14 are considered basic or basic.

Different plants have their own pH preferences. To ensure the best possible growth, you should be able to test the pH of the water and then adjust it.

For example:

- Cabbage likes pH 7.5
- Tomatoes as pH 6-6.5
- Sweet potatoes like pH 5.2 to 6
- Peppers as pH 5.5-7
- Salad and broccoli pH 6-7

In the rest of the book, we will explain why adjusting the pH is necessary.

You can get a pH meter at your local hydroponics store or online. You must calibrate the sensor with the calibration powder supplied with the reader. A basic pH meter costs $ 10 to $ 20.

Do not use paper test strips for water, as they are inaccurate. Usually, a pH meter is offered in combination with a TDS or EC meter, which we will discuss next.

EC meter

Electrical conductivity is a measure of the ease with which electricity flows through the water. The higher the ion content, the better it conducts electricity.

All water contains ions. Adding nutrients to water increases the ion content which effectively increasing electrical conductivity in the system.

EC or electrical conductivity is an essential part of the hydroponic equation. The easiest way to explain this is to use a guide to dissolved salts in water. Its unit is Siemens per meter, but in hydroponics, we use millisiemens per meter.

In short, the higher the number of salts in water, the higher the conductivity. Salt-free water (distilled water) has no conductivity.

Lettuce likes EC is worth 1.2 (or 1.2 millisiemens), while basil likes EC is worth 2.

For this reason, it is important to know the CE and what your systems prefer to make sure that your system is at the right level.

However, the weather also affects the requirements for electrical conductivity. When it is hot, the plants evaporate more water. This is why you should lower your EC during the hot summer months. During the colder winter months, you need to increase the EC.

- Reduce the EC on hot days.
- In cold weather, you need to increase your EC.

The EC meter does not release a certain amount of minerals or fertilizers into the water. If you are only using the right nutrients, do not worry.

It does not monitor individual nutrients; it does not mean it does not make sense.

They should generally be kept between 0.8 and 1.2 for leafy vegetables and between 2 and 3.5 for fruit crops such as tomatoes. The water source may affect the EC value. More on that later.

Sometimes you see the recommended nutrient levels listed, as CF. CF is the coefficient of conductivity. It is like EC, used in Europe. If you multiply EC by ten, you become CF.

For example, lettuce grows best in an EU of 0.8 to 1.2. It is CF from 8 to 12.

TDS meter

TDS stands for total dissolved salts. You may hear that some hydroponic producers refer to TDS rather than EC. Both are used to force your Hydroponic to determine. If you buy the TDS meter, you can also switch to EC measurements.

It is important to understand that TDS is a calculated number. TDS measurements are converted from EC measurements. The problem occurs if you do not know which calculation, method was used to generate the TDS. There are several of them.

In general, the EC and CF measures are used in Europe, while TDS is an American measure. Whichever measure you use, the two are actually the same: a measure of the nutrient content in your solution.

NaCl conversion factor

It effectively measures the salt in the water. The conversion factor for this mineral is the number of micro Siemens multiplied by any number from 0.47 to 0.5. You will find that most TDS meters use 0.5. It is easiest to remember and calculate. Most measuring devices sold to use the NaCl conversion factor.

For example, if you have a value of 1 EC (1 m Siemens or 1000 Micro Siemens), you have a TDS value of 500 ppm.

The natural water conversion factor

This conversion factor is called 4-4-2; it quantifies its content. This contains forty percent of sodium sulfate, forty percent sodium bicarbonate, and twenty percent sodium chloride.

Again, the conversion factor is a range, this time between 0.65 and 0.85. Most TDS meters use 0.7.

For example, one EC (1000 Micro Siemens) is equivalent to 700 ppm with a TDS meter that uses natural water conversion.

Potassium chloride, KCI conversion factor

This time, the conversion rate is not an area. It's just the number 0.55. The reading of your EC 1EC or 1000 Micro Siemens counter corresponds to 550 ppm.

These are not all the possible conversion options, but they are the most common. First, NaCl is currently the most common.

Dissolved oxygen sensor

Plant roots need oxygen to stay healthy and ensure proper plant growth. A dissolved oxygen sensor helps you understand the amount of oxygen available in the water and ensures that it is sufficient to keep the plants healthy.

If the plants do not bring enough oxygen to their roots, they can die. A minimum of 5 ppm is recommended.

A dissolved oxygen meter is expensive for an amateur, especially at first. For this reason, people who practice hydroponics for fun do generally not purchase dissolved oxygen meters. A good meter can cost between $ 170 and $ 500 for a reputable brand.

You do not have to invest in just one if you oxygenate the water. The water can be supplied with oxygen using an air pump with an air stone in the water tank. Depending on the culture method, you do not need to aerate the water.

The dissolved oxygen in the water is lowest in summer. The water heats up and the dissolved oxygen becomes less available. While your plants work very well in winter, there may be a lack of oxygen in summer.

Net pots

On some systems, you need containers to store the plants. This is especially true for deepwater cultures (DWC), Cranky, wick systems, aeroponics, nebulizers, Dutch buckets, and possibly vertical towers.

Make sure you have pots with an edge on top so they don't fall out. The standard size of lettuce is two centimeters (five centimeters). If you want to use tomatoes with Dutch buckets, 15 cm is recommended.

When building a new system on a budget, you can use many other options instead of buying net pots. For example, plastic cups with many holes or just a thin net on the frame. Use your imagination!

Humidity and temperature sensor

Estimating temperatures and humidity leads to errors. I recommend buying a simple humidity and temperature sensor so you do not have to guess. Most of them cost no more than $ 15.

Germination tray and dome

You have to start the seeds in a bowl of special germ. Most of these trays are 25 x 25 or 25 x 50 cm (10 x 10 or 10 x 20 inch) and usually contain a dome with moisture.

These bowls are used to germinate seeds and maintain high humidity. After the first true leaves appear, it is time to replant them in the system. This usually happens after ten to fifteen days.

The air humidity must be between 60 and 70%, while the temperature must be between 20 and 25 ° C.

Sowing starting cubes

If you're growing plants from seeds, you can't just put the seeds in mesh pots. They are washed away or sunk. Instead, you need the first to die. These cubes provide a place where the seeds can grow safely and the roots can grow.

When starting the seeds, various materials can be used as a growth medium:

Mineral wool

They consist of a combination of basalt and chalk which are combined. The result is a small cube that looks like cotton candy. Your seeds can be placed in a rock wool cube where they start to germinate. The cube goes into the net pot and your seeds should have everything you need to grow. Provided she has access to water rich in nutrients. These cubes come in all shapes and sizes.

You only need one, an inch and a half or a cube. Depending on the culture method, you may need to add growth medium to support the cube and block algae production by sunlight

You can separate each cube from a larger sheet. I recommend gloves because mineral wool can irritate the skin.

Like any seed starter, immerse it in water with a neutral pH of six before use. This guarantees a better seed germination rate.

Coco Coir

An alternative to rock wool cubes is coconut fiber

Coconut is an organic medium that decomposes over time. Some use it because it is ecological and renewable. I do not recommend starting with it. This can cause the system to hang and obstruct if you are not careful. It may start to rot somewhere and before you know it, you will deteriorate the quality of the water.

Oasis cubes

The next starting cube is the cube oasis. They keep moisture well and are very soft. This allows the roots to penetrate the soil more easily, but also to make them brittle. Oasis cubes are also used as a growth medium. These cubes are very popular in NFT systems.

Sponges

Sponges are mainly used as a cheap alternative to mineral wool or oasis cubes. However, they also do not absorb and store moisture. Therefore, using sponges is not a carefree method to start the seeds. They are not as ecological as the other initial seed cubes.

Growing media

After placing the seeds in the first seed cubes and they begin to germinate, you will see the roots emerging from the initial hubs.

It's time for you to transplant them to your second grow room. The media depends on the culture technique you use.

You don't need substrates for floating and NFT rafts. For other methods such as Cranky, Dutch buckets, or a wick system, it may be necessary to add growth media.

The use of growth media also depends on the size of the plant. Lettuce does not need a growth medium because it does not need support. Tomatoes need a medium to grow plants.

The growing media give your plant stability and root space for further development.

Hydro ton

These are the most popular harvesting media.

Hydro ton consists of clay heated to high temperatures. The result is a very porous material made up of small balls.

Hydro ton is very light, so your pots are not overloaded. It's great to keep the starter cubes in place. It is also easy to use.

Hydro ton should be washed before use to remove clay dust.

You can also sterilize these media again, but it can take time, especially if you have more than one.

Sterilization or re-sterilization is necessary because the medium may contain bacteria or other microorganisms that can be harmful to plants. Whether you are using it for the first time or reusing a growth medium, cleaning alone may not be enough to get rid of these bacteria. You must sterilize the medium to ensure safe reuse.

Sterilization uses heat or a chemical to kill all organisms on the growth media. Hydrogen peroxide is a popular chemical choice.

You need a thirty-five percent solution of hydrogen peroxide, then wash the clay balls thoroughly. Mix one part of hydrogen peroxide (thirty-five percent) with eleven parts of water. This reduces it to a three percent solution.

In particular, rinse the substrate several times to make sure that all traces of hydrogen peroxide have disappeared.

You can also use a ten percent bleach solution. The bleaching solution is also used to sterilize the NFT wells or other devices in your system.

An alternative is to heat the growth medium to 82 ° C (180 ° F) or more in an oven for at least 30 minutes. Pasteurizes and eliminates fungal microorganisms. To get rid of all organisms, you need to sterilize, which includes at least 30 minutes at 100 ° C (212 ° F).

Warning: doing this in the kitchen will leave a sour smell.

Nacre

If you take minerals and expose them to extreme heat, force them to expand and burst like corn, which effectively creates perlite. It is another medium with a neutral and extremely light pH. It is not good for storing moisture.

Gardeners in their soil to increase root ventilation use perlite. It is ideal for Dutch buckets (WKI yellow drops), the system reads in the introduction of humidity or Cranky methods.

You can buy Perlite at any garden store, but be careful not to get it in your eyes.

Use a dust mask when handling perlite. The dust that appears when handling perlite cannot be breathed in soundly.

Vermiculite

This silicon-based substance is exposed to the same high temperatures to form perlite. It expands and is very similar to perlite and also has a neutral ph. The main difference is that vermiculite has a high action exchange.

In other words, it is best to conserve water and nutrients for later release into the plant. Vermiculite is too good to store moisture to strangle the roots. This is why it is popular in a mixture of fifty and fifty with perlite.

Rockwool

As previously described, Rockwool is a great choice for starting seeds. Larger cubes of rock wool of a size of seven to fifteen centimeters can be used for the whole plant. Its pH is neutral and easy to use. Rock wool drains water very well.

Large rock wool cubes are mainly used for plants with a long life cycle. Planting lettuce in these large crops is not financially viable. The holes in these blocks are too large for the cuttings. You must use the Rockwool starter cube to grow seedlings, then transfer the plant to these larger cubes using the starter cube.

Another method of cultivation is to use rock wool panels. They are common on tomato farms. You can find these biggest rock wool media. You can put several large cubes of mineral wool on a plate. A plate is several feet long and is available in different sizes. These must also be soaked.

Do not remove the plastic cover from them. The plastic prevents moisture and light from entering. Drainage holes should be made at the bottom of the plate. Drip transmitters should be placed in large cubes of rock wool.

Grow Stones

Growth stones are made from recycled glass.

Growth stones are good for and water retention. That they (ten centimeters) can run above the water line at four inches of water.

The term glass should not dishearten you, they look like sharp edges, but they don't.

River rocks

As the name suggests, this type of culture comes from the riverbed. The stones are naturally rounded because the water removes the sharp edges. Due to the irregular shapes of the river rocks, there are many air pockets, which facilitate the fixation of the roots.

If you are using a hydroponic system at high and low tide, this may be the right choice. However, if you need more water retention, river rocks may not be the best option.

If your budget is tight and the hydro ton is a bit expensive, River Rock is the best solution. For best results, use a three-centimeter (two-centimeter) river rock.

River rocks should be washed before use to ensure cleanliness. If you plan to use it, keep in mind that this is an annoyance that may prevent you from moving your system in the future.

Pine shavings

It is not the same as sawdust, which absorbs water and blocks your order. Pine shavings should be made of oven-dried wood and should not contain any chemical fungicides. The best choice for buying this inexpensive growing medium is a pet store or carpentry factory nearby.

The larger the chips, the better the air pockets between them, which is good for the roots of your plants. Pine shavings are organic and disintegrate over time, making them a disposable medium.

Water absorbing crystals

You may have heard of them because they are used in diapers and many other products. They are not yet a common addition to hydroponic systems. They are also called hydrogels or superabsorbent polymers.

They expand and retain a large amount of water, which the plants can then absorb slowly. These crystals reduce or even eliminate air pockets. This means that your roots do not have enough oxygen.

To solve this problem, you need to mix fifty / fifty water-absorbing crystals with river rock or hydro ton. This creates water and oxygen

A pound bag costs about $ 15. Search for"Super *Absorbent Gel Granules* " or " *Water Storage Crystals* " *on the* Internet.

Remember to get pearls instead of powder. The powder will spoil. The size of the polymer increases as it is hydrated. Take into account the increase in size before transplantation. They are not a popular choice in hydroponics because of their price. They are only used with premium plants.

Some commercial systems use them in combination with peat moss for the first seed cubes.

Pump

The pump is an integral part of almost all hydroponic systems. This is responsible for the movement of water in the order and provides plants with the water and nutrients they need.

Although you will learn more about some systems that do not use a pump later in this book, most hydroponic systems do.

The size of the pump depends on the required flow rate and the pump head.

We will first look at the height of the head.

How tall is the pump?

Suppose you bought 250 gallons per hour of the pump. The pump tells you it's 250 gallons per hour, so it should pump 250 gallons per hour, right?

Not exactly

As you can see, the pump flow is described with a head height of zero (height). This means that the pump delivers 250 gallons per hour without lifting it into the system. The flow decreases when you start pumping water.

Fortunately, there are graphs for the pump that show the flow at a given height. In the image below, you can see such a curve, which is called the "pump curve." This curve shows the relationship between flow and head height in a helpful diagram.

Read the pump curve

Each decent manufacturer or seller has a pump curve in its user guide or datasheet. If you cannot find it on your website, search for "pump name + user manual." With any luck, you should see a PDF file with the pump curve.

After finding the pump curve, you want to use, first look at the left axis. Find the head height you have set for your system and draw a line to the right. Then find the minimum flow required and draw a vertical line. The intersection of these lines is the "working point" of the pump.

In this example, there are four hundred GPH pumps in the line.

If the operating point is between two pump lines, move to the right. Never go left as you will not reach the minimum recommended flow.

Imagine pumping 250 gallons per hour. The height is three feet. Draw a line in the head height diagram at the desired flow rate. The intersection of the two lines corresponds to the desired pump flow.

As you can see, a 250 gallon per hour pump would not have reached the level of 250 gallons per hour. It will pump one hundred and eighty gallons per hour.

Instead, choose a 400 gallon per hour pump if you want to pump at least 250 gallons per hour with a head height of 3 feet.

The simplest rule to keep in mind when purchasing a water pump, you can use the divided flow in the water tank to get the right flow of water. The pump flow cannot be increased if it is not strong enough. In other words, always buy a more powerful pump than necessary.

Let's look at the water requirements for different systems.

- ## Ebb and flow or flood and drainage

Thanks to the emptying and drainage technology, you flood the container and then empty it. The size of the pump depends on the size of the container and the height to be pumped. It usually takes five minutes to flood the tray with water.

Example: a trough of 2 x 2 x 1 foot has a square foot of 4 square feet. We are going to flood the plateau at 0.5 feet.

Convert two cubic feet to gallons:

The pump needs 15 gallons per hour to fill the suction cup. However, the general rule is that you have to pour the tray in five minutes.

You need a 180 gallon per hour pump to fill a growing container in five minutes. Remember, this is not the height of your head. You must specify the height of the head and choose a pump that delivers 180 gallons per hour.

The frequency of flooding depends on the growing environment. Mineral wool can be cast once a day, while Hydro ton takes several cycles a day. Rock wool water can last longer than a hydro ton.

- ## DWC (floating rafts)

You do not need a water pump for floating rafts. If you are using a tank to mix nutrients, you should have it to pump water from the tank into the floating troughs of the raft.

- ## Drops, Dutch buckets, NFT and vertical systems

If you use this type of system, use drip irrigation. The diameter of these drip lines is small, so no large flow is required. A 0.8 cm (3/8 inch) drop provides 30 liters per hour. You need to calculate the number of drip lines your system needs.

Example: The NFT system requires a drip line in a groove to reach the recommended flow rate of 0.5 liters per minute or 1/2 liter per minute. A 20-input system requires a pump with at least:

Conversion from liters to gallons:

Again, it will be regardless of the height of the head.

- **Aeroponic**

If you are using aeroponics, you need a high-pressure diaphragm pump. Aeroponicsis intended for advanced growers because it uses more technology than general cultivation techniques. Depending on the nozzles used, your pump should be at least 5.5 bar (80 psi). The flow also depends on the nozzles.

In the rest of the book, I will say more about aeroponics.

In many systems, the pump does not run continuously. The pump runs for a few minutes, which is controlled by a timer.

Timer

The timer is a small part and at the same times an essential element of any hydroponic system. Its job is to inform the pump or the lights when to turn them on and off.

It should be noted that a time counter is not required for each hydroponic system. NFT systems do not normally require a timer. Dutch bucket, drip and flood and drainage systems generally do this.

You can program the timer for the time you want to start the pump or the light. You can get mechanical and electronic watches. The mechanics are cheaper and can be adjusted at 30-minute intervals, ideal for lamps but not for pumps. Mechanical watches cost around seven dollars each.

For pumps, you need electronically adjustable timers. They have a display and intervals every second or minute. An electronically adjustable watch costs around fifteen dollars each.

Always read the rated power of each timer. It will not work if your devices consume a total of two thousand watts while the timer is only designed for one thousand five hundred watts.

Atomizer

You will not be surprised to learn that fog is a device that creates fog.

If you want to create a Fogponics cloning system, you need it. The smoke machine is also known as a smoke machine. It vibrates two million times a second and turns nutrient-rich water into a fog. It is then taken up by your plants and provides them with the necessary nourishment. The smoke machine floats on the surface of the water with a swimming device.

When you use a smoke machine, you usually need a lot of water or change it frequently. Indeed, the vibrations heat the water. Plants, especially maple, don't like hot water.

Aeration pump

The aeration pump adds oxygen to the water. You may be wondering why this is necessary since plants use carbon dioxide.

However, carbon dioxide is an essential part of the photosynthesis process, which generates energy for the plant.

Insufficient oxygen prevents the plant from carrying out basic processes that keep it alive. In general, when growing plants in the soil, you never have to think about oxygen levels. In a hydroponic system, however, you need to make sure that the roots are getting enough oxygen to meet their needs when submerged most of the time.

The exact level of dissolved oxygen (DO) depends on the plant you are growing and the temperature of the water. Most plants tolerate 5 ppm of dissolved oxygen. Lettuce needs at least 4 ppm. Harvest failures occur at values below 3 ppm.

We have talked about this before and looked at the dissolved oxygen sensor.

The pump disturbs the surface of the water, which causes movement. This movement allows the water to absorb more oxygen.

As the water temperature rises, the dissolved oxygen drops. You must ensure that the dissolved oxygen is always above the minimum recommended ppm.

If you have root rot, you should increase the aeration of the water. Dissolved oxygen increases root growth, which leads to more visible root structures.

The roots of an efficient hydroponic system are very different from those that do not receive enough oxygen. The roots with a lot of oxygen are white and have fine hair. Roots without much air are thicker and have fewer root hairs.

Heating mat

Your seedlings may need a heating mat when it is colder. This should help them germinate better. Set the heating mat to 25 ° C (68 ° F). A temperature above 25 ° C (77 ° F) has a germ-inhibiting effect.

The Root conditioner

The root conditioner helps young plants to develop their roots. It's optional, but if you're having problems growing slowly, gives it a try. It is mainly an organic brown liquid like humus root from simple growing solutions.

Dose for a simple root solution:

- One nut per liter of water or ¼ gallon.

Instead of placing the initial seed cubes in medium strength medium, you will also add nutrients to the roots.

Seeds

You need seeds to grow plants. It is better to use seeds; It is a seedling to buy from a dealer. The roots are dirty and should be washed before planting in the system.

Using seeds takes longer, but reduces the risk of soil diseases.

If you are using small seeds, you should buy granulated seeds. Granulated seeds are seeds covered with clay or other substances

The lights are growing

Depending on the installation location, you may decide that your plants use additional light.

Rising lights are the best way to do this because they have a light spectrum that plants love. The lights you get in a hardware store are for households and are unlikely to offer the desired intensity (lumens) or the desired light spectrum (Kelvin or PAR).

Light spectrum

In this image, you can see the light spectrum using the Kelvin scale:

If you choose a fluorescent lamp that brightens the light, you have two options. Purchase of cold blue lights (6500 K) or hot red lights (4000 K).

It is best to use a cool blue light for cuttings and vegetative growth. Plants use this light to generate energy for growth. Use them for leaf crops like lettuce, kale, basil, etc.

The second spectrum of light is a warm red light. It is used for growing fruit plants such as strawberries, tomatoes, etc. The red light makes the fruit that the plant produces large. If the plant does not have a red spectrum, the fruit produced is smaller.

Professional breeders use a combination of the two. They usually start with maple from a mature plant and put it in blue light. The spectrum of blue light stimulates the growth and development of the leaves.

When the plant reaches the desired leaves and shows signs of fruiting, it turns into a spectrum of red colors. The red spectrum is used to treat larger fruits.

The recent growth of medicinal plants will use the same technique. Instead of growing fruit, they form larger flowers with red lights.

If you use red light from the start, your plant will stretch and grow. In most cases, this is undesirable.

Here are the objectives for each growth phase:

1. **shoots:**

> Root growth
>
> Leaf growth

2. **Vegetative stage:**

> Root growth
>
> Leaf growth
>
> Stem growth

3. **Flowering period:**

> Create fruits or flowers

We have to adapt our light spectrum to each of these growth stages. The light spectrum is also called color temperature. The light spectrum or Kelvin should not be confused with PAR.

Light intensity

The light intensity is also important. The higher the light intensity, the more energy it provides to plants. The unit of light intensity is lumens.

The higher the light intensity, the more you have to hang it on the plant (less lux), which covers a larger area.

Some growing lights, such as expensive LED lights can reduce the light intensity for a certain spectrum of PAR light. It is used to switch one of the three steps mentioned above.

LUX

Lux is often confused with the intensity of light (lumens). They say that a lumen is a lux, which is not true. One lux is a distance per square meter.

Let's explain with an example.

The bulb has 1000 lumens. If I measured lumens with a lux meter, I would get different readings if I held it closer or further away. The more the lux meter is measured, the lower the lux.

If we were to use a 1000 lumen bulb and focus it on a surface of one square meter, we would get 1000 lux. If we spread the light over ten square meters, we would have 100 lux.

THROUGH

PAR or active photosynthetic radiation is the light that plants absorb in their different spectra. PAR light is used for photosynthesis of a plant. While the light spectrum (Kelvin) describes light for the human eye, the PAR indicates the type of light that each plant uses. For growing plants, the PAR is more precise than the light spectrum (Kelvin) because it is the spectrum that the plant sees.

PAR Daylight values

The PAR is displayed at the wavelength in nanometers (nm).

It varies from 400 nanometers, i. H. Blue, up to 700 nanometers, which is red.

Office and home designers use farmers Kelvin and PAR. Some lights grow, like B. T5 fluorescent lamps use the Kelvin scale to display the light spectrum.

In the previous image, you can see that the blue fluorescent lamps are not only blue, but also contain other colors that are not visible to the human eye.

Lighting time (photoperiod)

The lighting time depends on the system itself. Different plants have different lighting time requirements. For example, lettuce has a minimum recommended burning time of twelve hours a day. This means that your lettuce must be exposed to light for at least twelve hours a day to ensure optimal growth.

The duration of light during the plant's life cycle can change. For example, the lighting time when the tomatoes are growing differs from the fruit period.

PDF

PPF is a measure of the number of light photons per second that strike plants. PPF is called photosynthetic photon flux. Its unit is mol / s or micro molar per second.

When people measure PAR under a canopy of plants, they refer to the PPF. These terms are used synonymously at all times.

PPFD

PPFD or photosynthetic photon flux is a measure of the photosynthetic photon flux (PPF) at the surface. PPFD is expressed in moles / s / m^2 or micromoles per second per square meter.

PFD

The PFD or photonic flux density is the same as that of PPFD but has ultraviolet and deep red colors that are outside the standard PAR spectrum from 400 nm to 700 nm.

Recent research shows that wavelengths considered unsuitable for use by plants are beneficial for plants. However, they are outside the PAR range of 400 to 700 nm. The first P stands for photosynthesis.

PFD takes into account the whole spectrum instead of only PPFD. PFD is not used as often.

IDD

DLI or integral daylight is the amount of light a plant receives per square meter in a day. DLI is PPFD for that day. The DLI unit is micromolar per square meter per day or simply umol / m² / day. DLI is the amount of sunlight or artificial light received daily from the surface.

Each factory has a recommended DLI. If you grow outdoors or in a greenhouse, you can consult a map that shows the DLI in different parts of the United States.

You need a light source (solar or artificial) which supplies the system with the daily amount of DLI for a certain period of lighting. Any DLI that exceeds the recommended DLI would be a waste of energy as the plants are slightly saturated.

Light saturation is the point at which plants can no longer photosynthesize. This means that the plants can no longer absorb light per day or within a certain period (usually 24 hours).

Recommended DLI values:

- Leafy greens: 10-25 mole / m² / day
- Flowering plants: 25-35 mole / m² / day

To ensure that your system receives enough IDD, we calculate the IDD using an example.

IDD calculation

You must calculate your DLI to obtain the most efficient energy consumption and the greatest increase inefficiency. I'm going to use T5 fluorescent lettuce as an example to grow lettuce per square meter.

Lettuce likes DLI 12-14 mole / m² / day. Then we need to know how many lumens our growing light has. You can find it in the light datasheet. The one I use has 5000 lumens per four feet of T5 tubing.

Then we convert the lumens to PPF (photosynthetic photon flux), which gives us umoles / s (micromoles per second). I do this with the following calculator:

I choose a bright color, which is cold blue or daylight (6500 K), and I use lumens which emit a T5 light of 4 feet.

Convert PPF to PPFD

As we have a PPF of 115 µmol / s and an area of m², we do not need to convert it to PPFD. This is because PPFD is per square meter.

If we were to use these lights on two square meters, we had to divide them by two.

Then, 115 µmole / s = 115 µmole / s / m²

PPFD to DLI

Then we calculate PPFD (mole / s / m²) in DLI (mole).

Here is the DLI calculation formula:

4,968mol / m² / day is not enough for the salad to develop effectively.

We need at least 12 DLI for the salad to grow well. If I use more lights, I will reach the recommended IDD of twelve. Multiply DLI by three because I chose three T5 fluorescent lamps. We then become 14.9 mole / m² / day (3 · 4,968).

The IDD of 14.9 is a little too high, which will waste energy.

We now have two options:

- Increase lighting time
- Reduce the number of T5 tubes

In this case, I decided to reduce the number of T5 lamps and use two, because it is cheaper to buy two lamps instead of three and slightly increase the lighting time.

We recalculate the IDD

The final configuration would be to use two T5 tubes of 4 meters per square meter to grow lettuce every twenty-four hours with a light interval of fourteen and a half hours.

The T5 light consumes 54 watts per lamp. The total cost of ownership of this configuration would be:

Convert to kilowatts:

The national average is $ 0.12 / kWh. Calculate the cost per day:

Calculate the annual costs:

If we used three lamps and shortened the light interval, we would have similar electricity costs. I only buy two T5 lamps because two are cheaper than three are. The lamp itself is cheaper to replace (it has an average lifespan of twenty thousand hours = four years to two and a half hours a day).

You already have the sun in the greenhouses. This may be enough for the type of plant you are growing in the summer. However, if you want to grow plants in winter, you will probably need to supplement the light with lighting fixtures.

You will find that the IDD in Houston in December is 18.78 mol/day. If you are considering a greenhouse glass, you will get 16.9 mole / m² / day (90% yield).

- Glass: 90%
- Monolayer plastic: 85%
- Double layer plastic: 75%

While this is enough to grow lettuce, it would not be enough to produce fruit plants. Then you need additional lighting.

Suppose you want to reach 30 moles / m² / day in a greenhouse. Most greenhouses use MH (metal halide) in combination with

HPS (high-pressure sodium), which is interchangeable between the growth and flowering phases.

We have to add 13.1 mole / m² / day to reach 30 mole / m² / day (30-16.9).

I choose a light with a power of one thousand watts and I use average lumens for a light with metal halides of a value of one hundred thousand lumens. And choose a ceramic metal halide. Use the following converter:

We have an output of 1815 mole / s for this light. This light is very intense and can burn a plant if it is too close. So we have to increase the light (reduce the lux). When we raise the light, the surface increases. Let us say we are increasing the height to 4 m². We must consider this when calculating our DLI, because the IDD is measured in m².

Calculate the PPFD

We must divide by 4 in 1815 to cover all 4 m².

Then we have to use the formula to calculate the DLI.

Do you remember now that we needed an additional 13.1 mol / m² / day?

The harvest should be completed with eight hours of light from a thousand watts of ceramic halides distributed over an area of 4 m2.

Photosynthesis

Photosynthesis is a process that generates energy for a plant. This occurs in the plant and requires carbon dioxide, water and light.

This is something that only plants, algae and certain bacteria do. They take energy from the sun and convert it into chemical energy. Light energy transfers electrons from water to carbon dioxide, so plants use carbohydrates for growth energy.

Oxygen is a byproduct of this process, because carbon dioxide is used in the energy transfer process while water is oxidized.

Perhaps the most important thing here is not the chemical process that plants carry out continuously, but the fact that plants increase the amount of oxygen in the atmosphere.

You can now see why plants and trees are so important to our planet. They help create an atmosphere in which people can live. Another discovery we see and know from research is that increasing the level of carbon dioxide in the air accelerates plant growth. It also reduces the need for water and is more resistant to drought.

If your plant has limited or no access to the sun, then it might needs light with a light spectrum similar to that of the sun. While any light can be used to support plant growth, you should probably choose one of the options below for best results.

Fluorescence (T5.8 and 12)

You already know fluorescent lamps. It is no longer widespread in households. In commercial and leisure systems, they are used to start seeds. This type of light emits ten percent of its energy in the form of light and the remaining ninety percent in the form of heat. For this reason, you can place LED lamps closer to your awning than fluorescent lamps.

T5 is the latest most efficient fluorescent lamp on the market. The T8 and T12 are less efficient, but less expensive to buy. T5 is an excellent choice for growing indoor plants. Be sure to use a reflector returns light to plants.

Fluorescence is used to grow micro-greens and various plant plants. They have the right spectrum of colors (6500 K white light) for their culture. The 3000K color spectrum is also available. The fluorescence should be one foot (0.30 meters) above the plants and should be raised as the plants grow.

T5 is the preferred choice because it is the most economical fluorescent lamp. They come in different cases and come with a reflector and a chain for adjusting the height. They are ideal for beginners who want to grow plant plants.

They are also perfect for planting.

HID

High-intensity discharge lamps are widely used in commercial hydroponic systems. As their name suggests, they are mighty (high light intensity). You need an electronic ballast to turn on the light.

They form an arc between two electrodes in a closed chamber filled with gas, which emits the color indicated on the bulb. Most lamps have an E40 socket.

HID lamps can be divided into two subcategories:

- Metal halide (MH)
    - Ceramic metal halide (CMH)
- High-pressure sodium (HPS)

MH

The metal halide or MH is the best approach for growing plant plants such as large green leafy vegetables. The most common nominal powers are:

- 400 W.
- 600 W.
- 1000 W.

When growing flowering plants, you should use HD in the growth phase (leaves) and HPS in the flowering phase. You need a lamp that accepts conversion lamps so that you can change the lamps at the right time. This way you only have to buy one device. Do not touch the bulbs with your hands, use a cloth or towel instead. The oil on your hands can damage the light and shorten its life.

CMH

CMH or ceramic metal halide or ceramic metal halide is another type of metal halide lamp that is ten to twenty percent more efficient than a standard MH lamp. The purchase costs are higher, but the performance of this lamp outweighs the costs. After three years of working fourteen hours a day, you save $ 500 per CMH on MH.

HPS

If you have flowering plants, you should consider high-pressure sodium pear or HPS. It is available in the following nominal capacities:

- 150 W.
- 250 W.
- 400 W.
- 600 W.
- 750 W.
- 1000 W.

They give an orange-red glow and stimulate the flowering of plants.

Examples of flowering plants are:

- Tomatoes
- Eggplant
- Strawberries
- Cucumber
- Sunflowers

An HPS lamp should give you a five-year lifespan, but like any HID lamp, it will be less effective at the end of your life.

It is important to define the correct lighting configuration. If you hang it too high, lower your PPF. Too weak and the light becomes too intense and you will burn the plant.

A 1000 W light should be about 0.91 meters between the bowl and the bulb. It also depends on your reflector. If it is narrow, you should increase the height because the light is more focused.

The surface of the 1000 W light source must be 1.5 x 1.5 m (5 x 5 feet). So if you are using multiple lights, you should position them at a distance of 1.5 meters.

FROM HID

Double-sided high-intensity discharge lamps have two wires on both sides of the glass, which accommodate a double-ended tube. They are shorter and thinner than a normal tube. The result is a higher light density, which effectively gives your plants more light and a wider light spectrum (around 25 to 30% more efficient than single-sided bulbs).

In short, the double lamp reproduces the sun more effectively. They can be purchased in different PAR zones.

Of course, they are more expensive and this is a relatively new technology. Lamps should be handled with care and cannot be hung vertically. If you have a limited budget and want to use HID lamps, use double lamps.

FOLLOWED

LED lights are becoming one of the most popular options in many areas of life, and hydroponics is no different.

LED lamps to consume less energy than conventional bulbs, generally, last longer and have less heating power.

It is very easy to change the color spectrum when you want to switch to flower. Some LEDs have a fully adjustable spectrum, while others alternate between vegetative and flowering.

However, it should be noted that the purchase of LEDs is generally expensive and that their better efficiency in supplying the system with all types of light spectra is often exaggerated compared to HID.

The main advantage of LEDs over HID lamps is that they generate less heat and can have adjustable PAR spectra.

The light spectrum can only be adjusted for high-quality LEDs, which makes it more expensive.

CFL

Compactor compact fluorescent lamps are surprisingly inexpensive and a popular choice with many indoor growers. They are also a right choice for those new to hydroponics as they are one of the cheapest options available.

They are available in different lighting areas, but are less efficient than many other lighting options. This means that they must be close to the plants.

CHAPTER 1

DIFFERENT TYPES OF HYDROPONIC GARDENS

If we want to become a hydroponic gardener, we must first understand what options are available to us. In this way, we can choose a method that has advantages and disadvantages that correspond exactly to what we are looking for. For example, this means that if we do not want to risk clogging, we could avoid using pump-related methods. However, if we live in an area where it is difficult to control the amount of light around us, we can find a system that uses a pump, not one of the simplest, like deep-sea farming, where control light is also important. ,

Each of these systems offers unique advantages and disadvantages from which we can choose. But that does not mean that one system is better than the other. Like most things in life, choosing a hydroponic system should be based on your schedule, needs and skills. For this reason, I will not praise the benefits of a particular system. Instead, we will look at the most popular systems to determine their pros and cons. That way, you have the knowledge you need to choose the right type for you.

Drip system

This system is one of the most popular hydroponic sets but was invented for vegetable gardens in Israel. In the simplest simplification, the drip system uses a pump to get a drop of nutrient-rich water that feeds our plants. You can use less water by dripping slowly instead of spraying water usually in gardens.

The drip system generally consists of two key parts. The first is a nutrient-rich water tank that nourishes plants. At the top is a growing bowl in which our plants are planted. The pump is placed in water and connected to a culture bowl. From there, each plant receives its own drip line. This means that you use four drops when growing four plants on the same tray. Sixteen plants, sixteen drip lines. However, since we want to give the growing medium the substance you will use to replace the soil, it is time to breathe so as not to drown the plants. These drops use the timing system. The medium slowly returns the water to the tank, creating a closed system.

The drip system gives us excellent control over the amount of water and nutrients our plants receive. Thanks to this system, we can control the drop both in quantity and in length. This means that if we use too much water in the drip, we can reset it. or if our fall is too long or too short, we can adjust the counters we experience until we find the right length. One of the cool things about the drip system is that while it may take a while to get installed and running early, once everything is in place and we know our volumes, the system does not require general maintenance (depending on the specific configuration) like other methods. In addition, the materials required to make a drip system are not as expensive as some others are.

However, the drip system still uses the pump, and a clogged pump can decimate our gardens in just a few hours. Of course, it depends on the size of the system. Although the drip system is ideal for large operations, it can be too complicated for small operations.

The drip system works well for a variety of herbs and plants, from lettuce, onions, and peas to radishes, cucumbers, strawberries, and pumpkins. It turns out that these systems are fantastic for large factories. They also work best if you use a growth medium in which water flows slowly, such as peat or coconut foam.

So if you want to grow larger plants, the drip system is a good choice. Drip systems require a little maintenance and can be slow at first. However, once they work, they offer a high level of control over the growth process that any gardener would like.

Culture Deep Sea

Cultivation in deep water is considered the simplest hydroponic system and uses a reservoir system in which the roots of the plants are suspended. The plants sit at the top and instead of water drops; they just bend over to take the water they want. This makes the system SC mind easy to configure.

Culture on the high seas gets its name from the use of a deep reservoir and the depth at which the roots penetrate the water. Other systems, such as nutritional film technology, expose the roots of plants to air so that they can absorb a lot of oxygen. Thanks to this system, we place the growth tank above our tank and make sure that the material used prevents light from entering the system to prevent algae from entering the interior and spoiling the system. From there, the roots are suspended in the water and the water itself is oxidized with an air pump. This is done so that the roots do not drown in the water.

That is almost all. It was no joke that it is one of the simplest hydroponic configurations.

Deep-water cultures are ideal for this simplicity, but they are not the only advantages they offer. As there are so few moving parts in culture on the high seas, their maintenance is rather low. There is an air pump, but we do not pump water in this system, so the fear of losing gardens due to a faulty pump is not justified here. The simple configuration and less maintenance of these systems make them ideal for people who are entering the hydroponic garden for the first time and want to know if this approach is suitable for them.

Although the submersible culture pump is air, which causes fewer blockages, it is still subject to power outages. Since an air pump is necessary to supply oxygen to the water, a power failure can lead to the sinking of the garden. Depending on the size of the system, maintaining the pH in the water can be very difficult. With a smaller system, it is more difficult to make small pH changes because a slight overshoot or decrease can make a big difference in smaller. After all, it can be very difficult to maintain a balanced water temperature in these systems because we have to be careful when the tank is exposed to light.

Because of the way the system is set up, the suitability of deep-sea farming depends on several key factors when the plants are resting on the tank. The first key is the weight. If the plants we choose are too heavy from above, they can fall and break, and even move and lose the weight of the whole. No one wants a disaster to experience. Another important problem is that we have to choose plants that love water. This means that plants that prefer dry growing conditions do not work very well in crops on the high seas. Plants like lettuce, which like to absorb water, will love this system.

In addition to lettuce, herbs like basil and vegetables like kale, vegetables, sorrel, and sorrel are some good options for this system. Bok Choy and Okra also grow well in these systems and offer a variety that goes beyond traditional vegetables, which are considered garden vegetables.

Therefore, if you want to grow aquatic plants, deep-sea cultivation is an easy to install and low maintenance system. However, we have to be careful with the plants we choose. If they are too heavy or prefer dry conditions, the deep tank is not for them.

Food film technology

Thanks to the nutrient film technology, we re-use the water tank, but this time we pump it into a culture bowl arranged at a small angle. The execution of this on a way that way that the force of gravity so that in the rich parts water wit the ingredients for the desired nutritional Strewn field and ê starting from one end ñ Deputy compartment to the second, where ff ê then sp wit flows back into the tank. For more information on how we add nutrients to our water, see Chapter 4. Due to its design, this system is better suited for plants with a smaller root system. The NFT configuration is an active system.

Plants in the NFT system only have root tips that touch the water so that the roots can absorb precious oxygen that promotes growth. Because the system uses little water at a time, the plants are never melted in the water.

Due to the arrangement of the plants, it is very easy to check the roots of the NFT system for diseases. Using a self-referenced water tank reduces overall water loss and the system design makes it easy to scale the design to the size you need. Unlike deep-water cultures, it can also be fairly easy to determine the correct pH value with the NFT configuration.

However, NFT is also pump-based, so the risk of pump failure and crop decimation should always be taken into account. Because of the way the roots are cut in the system, they can block the flow of water. For this reason, plants with a large root system such as carrots are not suitable for the NFT system.

Since the roots are not really in the growing medium like the other systems we have examined, this means that the plants with the highest weight do not work here either. However, leafy vegetables like lettuce or fruits like strawberries have been very successful thanks to the NFT system.

Ebb and flow

For the system to work properly, you must set the pump to flood the compartment. We set this pump up on time instead of continually flooding it and melting the plants. The overflow pipe is positioned on the growth bowl so that the water returns to the tank. Depending on how we installed it, we can even turn on the air pump to make sure the roots get the oxygen they need.

The advantage of a drainage and drainage system is that the start-up is not expensive since obtaining the materials is not so difficult. The drain and drain system can be activated automatically after configuration. However, you still need to do maintenance to make sure everything is working properly.

It is important to know that this system is prone to failure. Therefore, we need to understand which areas of error are most affected.

One of the coolest things about the drainage and drainage system is that it can be configured to allow almost any type of plant or vegetable. Not so many plants that prefer a dry system, but the size is not a problem here, as was the case with the configuration of the nutritional film technology. Because it is so easy to build a structure; We can easily adapt it to the needs of our plants.

Evacuating

Of all the systems, we have and consider, the simplest way to wick is. It is so simple that it is often recommended as an entry point for hydroponics. The wick is a passive system with a very small number of parts; there are no water pumps in the wrong system.

In this system, we fill the water tank again and keep it under the culture bowl. This time, however, we do not use a hose to supply plants with water; we adopt an absorbent material such as a rope. This absorbent material is placed in water and wrapped in a growing bowl. Our tray is filled with a nutritious solution that absorbs and retains water well because this system works very slowly. Water flows through the wick to slowly feed the plants.

This system is ideal for its simplicity and can serve as an easy way to start hydroponics. It is also an inexpensive system, which greatly facilitates the investment of an inexperienced grower. Because there is no pump that could fail, this system is not exposed to premature death like pump systems. The absence of a pump also means that this system does not consume electricity and can be refreshing for those who worry about the number of their electricity bills.

Despite its simplicity, the drainage system still has drawbacks which we must take into account. The system does not provide nutrients, so plants that need a lot of water and nutrients are not very good. The system can also detect a toxic accumulation of nutrients in the nutrient medium if we do not pay attention to the amount of water absorbed and consumed.

Due to the lower water level in the absorption systems, they are better suited for small plants. Lettuce and smaller herbs are good for the brewing system, but water-hungry plants like tomatoes would not tolerate the brewing system. For this reason, the permeation system does not offer as much variety as the other systems. However, this lack of diversity is compensated by the simple configuration. The wick is an excellent system for those who will try hydroponics for the first time.

Aeroponic

The most complicated saved in the end. Aeroponics eliminates the environment and leaves the roots of plants exposed to more oxygen instead, which is why this system tends to grow faster.

In this system, the roots of the plants hang outside the container in which the system is built. At the end of the system is our nutrient-rich water tank. This time, however, the roots do not hang in the water. Instead, we use a water pump to spray the plant roots with a nutrient solution. This pump is of course configured in time to ensure that you do not overfeed the plants.

This system is ideal for the production of larger plants, as they do not have to focus on root growth. The absence of a growth medium also means that the roots do not have to hang; We provide them with nutrients directly. Exposing the roots to oxygen also promotes growth. This means that the aeroponic system is known to produce plants with impressive crops. This system doesn't take up much space either, so you can build it to be mobile enough. Due to the lack of growth medium, the aeropone system is fairly easy to clean.

We have to clean it because the constantly humid atmosphere of the system creates an environment in which bacteria and fungi can grow. The system is also very vulnerable to pump and power outages which, as we have seen, can be the main killer in our hydroponic gardens.

However, this system allows for higher yields and the system can be used to grow almost any type of plant. This means that the diversity of the aeroponic system is second to none compared to the other systems we have examined.

Choose the right system for you

Like many things in life, choosing a hydroponic system is very personal. Each of us has different goals in our gardens and various skills in dealing with technical matters. This means that the best option available to know which system to use is to ask questions according to our needs and desires, such as:

How can you create useful projects? If it is weak, it could be a perfect start to start with a percolation system. What plants do you want to grow? If you are looking for very heavy and large installations, you should use a system capable of handling them. If you're looking for something smaller, you have more options, but that doesn't mean you should get small if you're looking for a bigger plant. Do you have time to invest in one of the most demanding maintenance activities or is it rationalized, for example, B. Absorption, better suited to your life and garden goals?

Each configuration we examined in this chapter has been described on the Internet and has been the subject of extensive research. Many first-hand reports show how they were done. If you find it fascinating, you can do more and more research to make sure it's right for you. In research, however, it is striking that each has been used successfully and has been shown to grow extremely healthy and beautiful plants.

You know what you want more than anyone. If you look at the pros, types of plants and cons, you should have a good idea of where to start. I suggest that you limit yourself to the couple that interests you the most and from there.

Hydroponic Growth Systems

There are different hydroponic systems that you can use depending on your experience, available space, investment and the type of plants you want to grow.

Here are the most popular of them, how they work and how the system is configured.

Kratky's method

The Kratky method is the easiest way to grow your own crop. What makes this system so easy, especially for beginners, is the lack of pumps, electricity and even wicks.

The main advantage of this system is that the system starts automatically after its configuration. It is a "define and forget" system.

You need to:

- A glass, container or bucket of stone
- Sowing starting cubes
- Growth medium - Hydro ton works well.
- Net pots

It's anything but water, nutrients and a test kit.

Start

First, you need to prepare a seedling. Seedlings can be grown in the starting cube. Before transplanting, the roots must be visible at the bottom of the cube.

You can only use one plant per seed cube and one per net pot.

The Kratky method allows you to grow all types of plants, from tomatoes to lettuce. You need a bucket with a capacity of three to five gallons for tomatoes or cucumbers and a Mason jar or plastic bottle with a salad drink. I like to use wide neck glasses with 3 inch mesh pots.

Kratky's method is a harvesting and forgetting method that can be used on the windowsill. When the plant begins to grow, the level in the container drops. As the roots grow, they keep pace with the drop in water level. This continues until the plant is fully developed. Lettuce requires about 16 ounces of liquid (four hundred seventy-five milliliters), while a three to five gallon (eleven to eighteen liters) bucket often needs to be filled.

The roots absorb the water and the plant begins to grow. The nutrient solution drains, but the roots follow the drainage of the water.

The empty space created supplies the roots with oxygen. This continues until the plant is completely ripe and the water stops flowing. You should strive for plant growth to follow the water in the tank.

You should place the setup in a well-lit environment. You should darken the outside of the container with aluminum foil. This is to prevent the algae from growing in the container. Do not use black paper or paint, as this will heat the water in the container.

If the water has completely drained and the plant is not yet fully developed, you need to refill it. You have to fill it in half so that only half of the roots are submerged.

This system can be installed almost anywhere and takes up very little space. I recommend this configuration for all those who start with hydroponics.

Create a system

Smaller plants:

Take a two or three inch pot of mesh and put a little hydro ton on the bottom. Place the seedling with the starting cube in a mesh pot. Fill the sides with a hydro ton to keep the cube in an upright position. Pour the nutrient solution into the container until it touches the bottom of the original seed cube. Darken the water tank so that no algae develop inside.

The image below shows many places where plants can grow with a container.

Larger plants:

Use a three or five gallon bucket and a 6-inch pot with a lid. The process is the same as for a smaller installation. A 6-inch net pot becomes easier for the plant because the root system is much more important.

When you fill a buckct, fill it halfway. This is to ensure that the roots have access to oxygen. If you submerge the entire root system, root rot occurs and your plant dies.

Wick system

The wicking system deserves second place in terms of hydroponic systems that are easy to implement.

It is so simple that it has no moving parts and is not dependent on electricity.

It is a simple system to build that introduces hydroponics. It is very similar to the Kratky method, but with a wick.

You will need

- Plastic bottle or bin with lid
- Two-inch pots
- Sowing starting cubes
- Increasingly chosen media
- Drainage rope

Structure of a wicking system

The premise is simple. Your water tank contains the water and nutrients your plant needs. At the top is the plant and the conductive cord, which provide the plant with water and nutrients through the capillary action of the wick.

First, drill two-inch holes in the top of the cover. Drill as much as necessary to fill the top of the lid. Remember that your seedlings will grow. Consider it. Lettuce should be six to eight inches (center to center) depending on the variety.

First, fill the container with water and a nutrient solution.

Take 2 cm pots with a net and place a tray with a string so that it touches the growth medium. Make sure it touches the roots of the plant you wish to place.

Put the lid on the container and place the mesh cups in the drilled holes. The wick is in aqueous solution. When used properly, the wick provides nutrient-rich water to the roots of the plant. Let this wick touch the bottom of the water tank. When the water flows slowly, the wick provides water to the roots.

It should be noted that this is a good system for small plants like lettuce and herbs. However, it is not very practical for more common plants such as tomatoes, fruit plants and peppers. You usually need a lot of water and nutrients. The wick system may not deliver them quickly enough.

If you choose to create a wick system, you should carefully consider the material of the wick. It is worth testing and always soaking them first to get the most effective absorption effect.

The best option I have found is to use a thick candleholder. They are used to drain the wax and are made of cotton. They are also quite thick. A six-foot throw costs $ 6. You can also reuse them.

You can make a tank as large as you want and increase the number of your plants.

It is also important to remember that the wick evenly absorbs water and nutrients, but not your plant. When the air is warmer than usual, the plant evaporates more water than when it is colder. Evaporation leads to the absorption of nutrients from the wick. This can cause nutrients to build up on the wick, which affects its ability to function effectively. Therefore, you should wash or rinse the wick after each harvest to remove excess nutrients (buildup of nutrients).

Make sure that the sun or the rising light does not enter the water tank. Wrap something around it so that light does not enter the container and does not form algae in nutrient-rich water. Aluminum foil is perfect for this. Avoid using black spray paint as this will heat the water in the container.

Alternative

If you want an even simpler method, you can use a plastic bottle and cut the lid. Turn the top of the bottle at the bottom and insert a moisture wicking cord with the bowls. You can leave the plug and drill a hole in it or remove the plug completely. You should keep an eye on the tank as it drains quickly.

Ebb and flow

This is another easy system to set up, but it should be noted that it is mainly used to operate the seeds.

With growing experience in hydroponics, you will likely continue to use seeds in this system and then transplant them into a different configuration. Commercial companies use this technology for sowing.

The drainage and drainage system is also called flooding and drainage, simply because the roots of the plant are flooded for a few minutes and then drained again.

The point of the flooding and drainage cycle is the exposure of the roots to air, while the hydrating growth medium continues to provide water and nutrients to the seedlings. Nutrients for cuttings are recommended to be halved, as they are sensitive to nutrients. More on this later in this book.

Pouring and drying are carried out automatically with the clock.

You will need

- A container for your plants
- Water reservoir
- Pump, preferably submersible
- Pump timer
- Pipes for pumps
- Siphon of your choice
- Your choice of growth medium

The planter is located above the water tank. The pump floods the plant tank at the defined level, and then returns through the overflow pipe to the tank.

The timer stops the pump and the water returns to the tank through the outlet side of the pump.

Design system

First, drill two holes in the bottom of the planter. A hole is used to supply water to the tray the other acts as a transfer.

Put water and nutrients in the water tank and turn on the pump. You can specify the time it takes to fill the plant container before it overflows. When the pump is stopped, the water returns through the pump line to the water tank and creates a drain and a flow.

It should be noted that sunlight or artificial light is likely to enter your father's flooding and drainage into the water. You should remove algae regularly to make sure that no dissolved nutrients and oxygen are used for the plants.

After the timer starts, water is pumped from the tank into the tank.

The water reaches the overflow and returns to the water tank. Remember that the

When the stopwatch stops, the water returns through the pump to the tank.

You can also use a different flood and drainage system. It uses the overflow and slow return of water to the tank.

Alternative flood and drainage system

This system uses a single hole in the flood tank. Water is pumped into the timer as in the previous method. When the table is flooded with water, it can return to the tank in a vertical pipe.

The diameter of the overflow pipe must be large enough to return the overflow to the water tank.

When the water reaches the desired level, the stopwatch must stops. The pump stops and the water stops flowing. The water still in the pickling tank slowly flows back through the small hole at the bottom of the overflow pipe in the water tank. This small hole slowly returns the water to the tank.

The hole must be small enough for the water to flow into the vertical pipe. The height of the standing pipe determines the water level. The water slowly returns to the tank.

DWC system

Most people will try the Kratky system and wick before using this system.

It is a deep-water culture or a DWC system. In some ways, this is very similar to the Kratky system, except that the roots of the plants are constantly submerged in water.

This system is always equipped with an air pump. Each system in which the roots can rest directly in the water is called standard water cultivation. To be considered a deep-sea farming system, the water must be at least 30 cm deep. The depth of the water serves as a temperature buffer.

There are two main DWC systems:

- DWC bucket (amateur)
- Floating rafts (commercial systems)

We will begin to explain the 5 gallon DWC bucket.

You will need

- Five gallon bucket or larger container
- Lid with 6 inch mesh pot
- Sowing starting cubes
- Air pump
- Air pump flexible hose
- A cornerstone
- Your growth medium (hydro ton is preferred)

Design system

Before you start building a DWC hydroponic system, think about what you are going to grow. Medium plants such as tomatoes or peppers are best suited for the DWC bucket system.

You should cut or drill a small hole in the top of the bucket. It must be large enough to hold a flexible air hose. The hole is drilled in the top of the bucket, not in the lid. This facilitates the occasional removal of the lid to check the water level and the roots.

Now place an air stone at the bottom of the water tank.

You can now connect your airline to the air stone and the other end to the pump.

Use a 6-inch mesh pan lid that fits in a standard 5-gallon bucket. Place the washed growth medium (hydro ton) in a mesh pot and place the seedling in the middle.

Large 15 cm mesh pot that fits in a 5-gallon (18 liters) bucket

You can now fill the bucket with nutrient-rich water. You are about to immerse the root base as with the Kratky method.

Once you have done it right, you can draw a line directly above the water line in the tank. It is advisable to draw a few lines around the container. This ensures that the lines don't just wear out. These lines are used as a reference to fill the container during emptying.

Do a final nutrient and pH check and put the lid back on the plant in a mesh pot.

If your bucket is in the sun, you should wrap it in aluminum foil to prevent algae from growing. Do not paint it black because the water in the bucket heats up quickly.

Algae need three things to thrive: light, nutrients, and water. You have to block the light in the water to remove one of these things from the equation and reduce the likelihood of algae.

Tip: when trying to remove and remove the cover to check the pH, etc. Make a small hole in it and draw water with a pipette to test. A small hole makes it easier to fill the water if necessary.

The image below shows four segments that use this system. I would improve the configuration by drilling a small hole in the bucket myself instead of passing the air hose through the mesh tray.

If you want smaller plants like lettuce, you can use a bathtub as in the following example:

I have already mentioned that there is another culture method on the high seas which is mainly used in commercial systems. These are called floating rafts.

Hydroponics in floating rafts use polystyrene rafts that float on water. As with the bucket system, the roots are soaked in water and air from the stones are placed underneath.

The polystyrene material must be food. Most foam insulation boards have a fire resistant coating that penetrates and contaminates water. Look for the blue DOW foam sheets.

When building this system, do not expose the water to concrete as this changes the pH of the system. Instead, choose a 0.5mm gasket insert.

Floating rafts can only be used with small crops like lettuce. The larger the plant, the more difficult it is to lift the raft and the more space it takes up.

You can also use the floating raft technique in your home system. You can do this by cutting out an IBC bag or using a bathtub.

The advantage of culture on the high seas is that the temperature remains stable due to the large volume of water. As the water drains, the floating rafts sink with the water level.

Drip system

You may have encountered a drip system with conventional potted plants. It is a very popular option as it is very easy to add or remove plants and automate the system.

The principle of this type of hydroponic system is to provide the roots with nutrient-rich water by making it flow slowly over the roots of plants.

There are two methods for drip systems:

- Recirculation
- No upheaval

Most drip systems are designed as circulation systems. The circulation system pumps water from the tank to the systems and have a drainage system through which water can flow back into the tank and the water can flow efficiently.

This is an effective approach because the loss of water is minimized and only what is released by plants or evaporates into the atmosphere is lost. You need a minimum amount of water to replenish the system.

However, the non-circulating system does not leave water in the tank. For this reason, they are also called "Run to Waste" systems.

This may seem like a waste because the water must be replaced regularly. However, it is a very popular option for commercial farmers as the costs involved are low.

The circulation less system works with the additional tank. The supply of nutrient-rich water is precisely measured so as not to lose water and nutrients. This minimizes losses.

You should mix the next batch with a given ratio of nutrients and water.

Drip systems are used in various systems, such as:

- Watering bowl
- NFT
- Dutch bucket
- Vertical towers and frames A.

First, I explain how to create a drip irrigation system on a tray.

You will need

- Large planter
- Water reservoir
- Submersible pump
- Timer
- Drip irrigation materials (listed separately)
- Growing media

Design system

The system uses a pump to create pressure in the irrigation hose.

The irrigation hose is a standard garden irrigation hose that you can buy at your local hardware store, for example. B. Home Depot or Lowes. You need the following for a drip system:

- Main pipe: ¾ inch (1.9 cm) pipe
- Second line: 0.6 cm tube
- Stroke
- Drippers
- Emitter rate (2 per plant)
- Etude inch (1.9 cm) hose closure

If you do not want to use end cards or sliders, you can use the T-divider and create an endless loop.

When setting up the system, use a large compartment to place the pots. You can use a professional potting soil as shown in the image below. A cheaper alternative is to create your own using a plastic insert.

This bowl is used to collect the drain of the emitters drop by drop. It collects the water and returns it to the nutrient tank.

The image below shows the configuration with the system without circulation or waste disposal.

Remember: The better the water retention of the growing medium, the more tolerant the plants in case of delayed watering or other problems. I recommend using Rockwool.

How to install a drip transmitter

Draw a drip line on the plants and drill the two holes next to each plant. Insert the drip heater and connect it to the irrigation line. Then add the drip rate.

The excess water crosses the ground and lands on the plateau. From there, the water comes back or is removed from the bowl.

The pump is connected to a timer, which should run three to five times a day for five minutes.

The next step is to fill the water tank and test the system. If you are satisfied, add plants and nutrients.

NFT

NFT stands for Nutrient Film Technique. This is another simple project, but it is especially useful when growing lettuce or other fast growing plants.

However, it should be noted that this type of system uses flat pipes or gutters. Plants with extended roots can block the flow of water and cause problems.

There are many different designs of the NFT system, but the basics are the same. Nutrient-rich water is pumped along gutters around the system, where plant roots can touch the water and extract the necessary nutrients. The water flow must be constant and the channel must be flat.

You will need

- Nutrient solution tank
- Submersible pump
- NFT channels
- Return pipes
- Drip irrigation parts

How to build it

First decide where to place your tank. It is the most difficult part of the system to move. Then you can take your first piece of gutter and drill two inch holes on one side every eight inches to get lettuce (upside down). If you are using flat gutter pipes, you can drop the starter cubes directly into the sewer without mesh pots. If you are using a round tube, you will need a mesh pot to hold the seedling in place.

Place the gutters on the frame with a drop of four degrees. You can place multiple channels side by side.

Then add the return line to the water tank. The return line can be placed under the gutters for simplicity.

Although this system provides plants with nutrient-rich water very effectively, plants suffer quickly if the water flow is disrupted for any reason.

The film must be very thin. Do not create a DFT system (Deep Flow technology). The advantage of the NFT system is that the water does not require additional aeration because the roots have access to oxygen.

In the United States, you can buy a gutter that lies flat at the bottom. The 3 x 2 inch down pipe is ideal for the inexpensive NFT channel. The holes must be spaced 20 cm apart so that the lettuce heads can grow. Start with ten centimeters on the side and then eight centimeters between the following holes. Leave a space of 20 cm between each NFT channel.

The main PVC pipe behind the pump must have a diameter of 3 cm. From there, go to a PVC pipe 1/2 inch in diameter (a point nine centimeters). From this point, nine centimeters, drill holes to accommodate the drip lines. Use a maximum of 10 drip lines for each 1/2 inch PVC pipe.

Drill 3/8 inch holes with a drill and use 3/8 inch eyelets to hold the wires in place. The outer edge of the supply line presses against the eyelet, which leads to a tight seal. The supply line consists of a 3/8 inch drip irrigation hose and has a flow rate of 0.5 liters per minute per hose.

Internet users suggest that the best flow rate for NFT hydroponics is one to two liters per minute. However, studies show that a flow rate of 20 liters per hour or 0.33 liters per minute gives the best performance. Read the study:

Dachrinnenart

On commercial systems, you only see flat channels. This widens the contact area with the roots to absorb water. Most homebuilders use a 3 inch downpipe.

You can reduce the flow when working with cuttings, and then gradually increase them as the plants grow.

Dutch bucket

The Dutch bucket is another drip system that is ideal for growing plants with more pronounced root structures such as tomatoes, cucumbers or peppers. It is easy to repair and more buckets can be added in the future if necessary.

Before you start creating a Dutch bucket system, you should understand the difference between drip systems and the Dutch bucket system.

The two systems are largely the same: both the feed water and the plant nutrients through a drip system. The main difference is that the Dutch bucket system uses buckets, usually three to five-gallon buckets, hence the name. Producers prefer the circulation of the Dutch bucket. This means that the excess water will return to the main water tank.

No other configuration is in circulation. This occurs when the water flow is correctly dosed so that no return line to the water tank is necessary. Non-circulating systems are cheaper to build but require a different dosage of nutrients than circulation. The correct dosage of nutrients in circulation less systems can be found on the manufacturer's website for the individual nutrients you are using.

Let's create a complete drip system for a Dutch bucket. You can find all the parts you need at your local hardware store.

You will need

- Three, four or five-gallon pails
- Non-sealable single-wall connectors or blade guides
- Culture media-perlite, river rock, or a combination of both
- Water tank with a capacity of at least 15 gallons (depending on the system)
- Submersible pump
- Plastic main pipe and ¼ inch pipe
- Some bricks and wooden planks
- 8-gallon drip heater (2 per bucket)
- One inch bend to drain
- 1 inch PVC pipe for drainage
- Two inch PVC pipe for the main drain

Start

First, you need to estimate the height of the Dutch buckets. You must bring the buckets of nutrients in the water tank by gravity.

Then place several stones above - above prepared by others and create an area where you place a bucket k with the advice of the box L au above the sea bridge between the stones to join.

You must drill a hole seven inches from the bottom of the bucket. Use an inch saw a hole in the bed and clean the SC - paper - friction edge. In ¼ of an inch-unseal and bedding in the hole.

The next step is to connect all the buckets to the main drain line. It will be a 2-inch PVC pipe. You have now returned to your water tank.

Then we have to create a flow of water in the buckets. We do this with a half-inch irrigation hose made of poly tubing. Run to the buckets and hit the hole all at once, like a normal drip system.

Place a quarter inch of the irrigation hose in this hole and run it in Dutch buckets. Then add 2 gallons of emitter drop by drop and place it near the root of the plant. If your buckets are white, add aluminum foil to prevent sunlight.

Perform a leak test before adding the media. If there are no leaks, you can put washed media in the bucket.

It is important to note that the pump does not have to run continuously: it should last fifteen minutes three to four times a day, although you can change it depending on the local temperature. If the substrate dries quickly, extend the time.

Simple cleaning tips:

After collecting the fruits of the plant, stop the flow of water in the Dutch buckets. Let the plant soak for a few days to absorb all the moisture from the bucket. This facilitates subsequent cleaning.

Store the perlite in a mesh bag so that it is separate from the river rock or hydro ton. This facilitates cleaning and separation after harvest.

Vertical system

The vertical hydroponic system saves space and can be manufactured in many different form. Vertical system A uses NFT channels for plants, while vertical towers use custom growth towers or 3-inch PVC pipes. Both use drip irrigation.

Vertical frame A.

Of course, you do not have to be small. The following design measures six feet by ten feet. You can grow one hundred and sixty-eight plants in this room!

You will need

- Wood for frame A
- Drain hose twelve by three inches nine feet long
- Three inch gutter pipe supports
- Unseals or three-quarter inch guides
- Quarter inch poly tubing
- Pump
- 3/4 diameter pipe for drain pipes
- The container as a water tank

Start

Start by creating frame A. You will need a four-foot piece of wood, then two pieces of wood tied and connected at the top. This creates an A-frame at each end. Medium support is also a good idea. Then you need to connect the two ends with several wooden slats, three or four on each side.

You can also add braces to make sure it is a solid, self-contained A-frame.

You can now install the gutter clips on one of the lower posts. You want three supports on each post to support six gutter tubes. It is important that they descend four degrees. Do not allow water to enter the sewer system. Otherwise, use the DFT system (Deep Flow technology). The DFT system is a DWC system in the NFT system.

Now you can cut two-inch holes in PVC pipe to contain mesh pots: you should have twelve PVC pipes, each measuring nine feet; six on each side when the distance between the plants is eight inches

Place the PVC pipes in the clips and insert mesh pots into each of the holes. You can use Rockwool or alternative supports in pots ready to plant.

You should also put a plug on the gutter to prevent water from escaping. You can do this by removing the end cap so that it is easy to clean when needed.

Your submersible pump must enter the tank. From now on, you should connect the pipes to the center of your A-frame. From now on, you will use the same visa as those used in NFT systems.

Then you need to add a small valve to the irrigation hose to control the water flow. This is used to regulate the flow because the lower line extracts more water than the upper line due to gravity and drag. Adjust the flow of twelve flexible lines so that the flow in each channel is uniform.

You must test this part of the system before adding seeds, cuttings or plants. Select a pump according to the instructions in this book.

The pump should run continuously. It is important to remember that the more levels you have in a vertical arrangement, the higher the pump power required, the higher the head height.

Vertical towers

Hydroponic towers are another option to consider. You have to decide how many spins you want. This is directly related to your budget and the space available.

The seven-foot pipe contains nests for twenty plants. Therefore, if you start with six tubes, you have enough space to grow 120 plants.

The great thing about this tube is that it takes up little space. You need to create a frame that will support the pipes. You can make these pipes yourself by creating a space in the PVC pipes, heating them with a heat gun and inserting a mold (2-inch pipe) the size of a pot with a grid when the plastic is still hot.

Water is routed to the top of the towers and flows through the sump to the tank (comparable to Dutch buckets).

The towers must be attached to the chassis. You can make this frame with wood and metal wire. You can attach these towers to the chassis.

As with the NFT A-Frame system, you must use a 3/4 inch irrigation hose as the main hose and attach a smaller irrigation hose to the towers.

You can increase the water distribution with a wick in a vertical tower.

Aeroponic

Aeroponics is a great way to use hydroponics in a futuristic way. I only recommend aeroponics if you already have experience in hydroponics. Aeroponics is not easy and many things can go wrong, for example, B. clogging of nozzles. Aeroponic systems are popular for cloning.

There are two types of aeroponic systems. The first to discuss is the low-pressure system. Then we will talk about the high-pressure system.

Low-pressure system

The low-pressure system is not a true aeroponics. With low pressureaeroponics, you do not create the sensitive fog created by high-pressure aeroponics. However, amateurs find an alternative to expensive high pressure systems.

This system, used by many amateur producers, is a plastic drum with a capacity of fifty-five gallons. Holes were made in the drum to accommodate the 45-degree elbows. The elbows correspond to the pots with a grid for your plants.

The roots begin to grow inside the barrel, where they are regularly sprayed by garden jets, which are pressurized by the pump. Water flows from the barrel to the tank, where it is easy to mix nutrients and measure their level.

You need to choose a pump that can create pressure in the system. Remove the flow from the nozzle and multiply it by the amount you have on your system. Also, consider the height of the system head. Lift the pump at least twice to reach the desired pressure.

Example:

They have ten nozzles with a flow rate of 30 gallons per hour at 20 psi each. You would need a pump that could deliver 300 gallons an hour regardless of the height of the head. Multiply it by two because we need pressure in the pipes. It will be 300 gallons per hour x 2 = 600 gallons per hour.

Then we look at the height of the head. In this example, it is four feet. Next, we first draw a horizontal line, then a vertical line at a speed of 600 gallons per hour. We see that we have to use a 1000 gallon per hour pump.

The nozzles are ordinary garden nozzles. Be sure to use 180-degree spray nozzles. It's forty-five and ninety degrees, but they don't wet the whole barrel. You should use garden sprinklers (plastic) instead of brass nozzles. Brass nozzles are only intended for high-pressure systems.

High-pressure system

High pressure aeroponics is an effective technique that allows the roots to access oxygen for healthy growth.

A high pressure system costs more than a low pressure system and is mainly used in commercial homes or cloning machines.

Each high-pressure aeroponic system consists of four key elements:

1. Pump

In many ways, this is the heart of your system. Without them, you will not get the haze effect you need. The pump increases the pressure in the system so that the spray nozzles work properly.

An excellent guide to pump pressure is to make sure your pump can deliver at least 4 to 5.5 bar (60- 80 psi). The mounting nozzles do not operate at a pressure below this. The pumps used are diaphragm pumps.

Your pump should be designed for high pressure. No pump is running. Most pumps have an integrated pressure switch. The pressure switch stops the pump at the highest pressure for which the pump is designed. If there is no pressure switch, the diaphragm of the pump breaks and the pump becomes unusable.

The pumps used in high-pressure aeroponics are self-priming pumps.

2. Pressure vessels

You have probably seen the pressure tank in your domestic water system. They help maintain water pressure.

There are two segments in the tank: a bladder and compressed air. Water fills the tank, thickening the air and increasing the pressure on the bladder. This keeps the pressure on the system. The water flow in the tank regulates the pressure.

It acts as a pressure buffer so that the pump does not need to be turned on and off every few seconds. You don't need it, but it's much better for the life of the pump.

3. Fog on the nozzles

Spray nozzles have small holes called openings. They are only 12,000 centimeters! In this system, the best idea is to have 10,000-inch holes.

The fact is that the pressure of the water flowing through the mist nozzle turns the water into mist. This mist is then sprayed on the root zone of the plant and provides it with water, nutrients and oxygen. In short, everything you need.

4. Filtered

The opening of the spray nozzle being small, the filters prevent clogging. A 30 micron filter is sufficient to avoid clogging the nozzles.

It should be noted that the plants rest on the box with roots in the box. The mist machines are in the box and there must be a drainage point so that the water can return to the water tank in which the pump is located.

Fogponics

Fogponics works much like Aeroponics, but this type of system uses fog instead of fog. Mainly used to create clones. An ultrasonic device that floats on the water generates the mist. The vibration evaporates the water.

This brings us to its main disadvantages:

- The water in the tank heats up.
- The container must be closed so that the mist remains trapped in the container.

To create a Fogponics system, you need:

- Tank
- Ultrasonic vibration device
- Pots or necklaces for cloning

The small storage container that holds ten gallons is perfect for this set. You need it with a lid that you can close.

You will need to drill several 2⅛ inch holes in the lid to insert pots with a net. If you are using this cloning system, these holes can be brought together. If you are using it for lettuce, you should use the correct distance between the plants (about 20 cm).

If you are using clones with mesh pots, you need to cut the bottom of the pot mesh. This is used to adapt the maple stem to the case. If you have special clone pots, you don't have to because there is a hole at the bottom.

Then use a foam insert or a collar that stays in place and the mesh shell does not fall into the tank. The maple stem slides through the foam and protrudes into the bag (but not submerged). Ideally, you need two knots under the clone collar. The knot is where the leaves appear on the stem.

You need to cut an additional hole to wire the ultrasonic fog. You can cover the hole with clone foam around the cable so that the fog does not escape.

Then you need to add a smoke machine. Look for fog that throws at least 400 ml of water per hour into the air. Consumes about fifteen to twenty watts. After connecting the smoke machine, you can use the start time and a one hour break. No pump is required for this system.

You should check your water level, nutrients and temperature regularly.

CHAPTER 2

HOW TO BUILD YOUR OWN SYSTEM

Now that we know the different types of hydroponic configurations we have, it's time to see how they are constructed. We will look at three different configurations that are best suited for beginners. As we have already seen, each system has its advantages and disadvantages. This means that the system you have chosen meets your needs. In this chapter, however, you can also determine which configuration is right for you, depending on the difficulty.

Although there are many sites and companies that sell hydroponic kits, it can be very easy to make them yourself. This does not mean that the sets purchased in the store have no value. Before spending a lot of money, however, DIY sctup can be a great way to master the basics of setting up a hydroponic garden. Once we know what we are doing, we can add different types of devices and devices to customize and align our gardens. But we have to start somewhere and DIY is a great place to start.

Drip system

For this system, we are looking at one of the easy-to-build drip systems. Here, buckets are used for growing plants that still receive nutrient-rich water through a series of tubes. To implement this project, we need to build three key areas: buckets, tanks, and pipes. We will see what you need to do to create a configuration with a single installation, but we will see how easy it is to customize the system to include more.

Start with a bucket. For our purposes, we will start with a 5-gallon bucket, but you can increase or decrease it if necessary. The first thing we do is to tip the bucket so that we can easily reach the ground. We want to configure the drainage so that the water flowing in the system is returned to the tank. We use a continuous fitting for this purpose. These little guys are used in different fields and you can easily pick one for a dollar or two at any hardware store.

Place the through hole at the bottom of the bucket, touch the side of the wire and screw it around. This should give you a small circle at the bottom of your bucket. We want this circle to be closer to the edge than the middle because our bucket should rest comfortably on a raised surface. When this is done, cut out the circle and place the hole in the bucket. Tighten the hole. A drain is now installed in your bucket. Take a filter, which may be an oven filter or whatever, and cut it out so that it rests on the hole in the bucket. This helps maintain water drainage, not our substrate.

Before going to the next step, we need to paint the buckets. We can double this task and paint our tanks at the same time. Use black paint on the outside of the bucket to block the light that would cause algae growth. Buckets painted black attract a lot of heat, which would increase the temperature of our water and can be a real long-term problem. For this reason, it is recommended to apply one or two white colors to the black color so that they reflect and do not absorb light.

We will use a similar design for our tank, but the main difference is that the cut hole is at the top, not at the bottom. After painting the tank in black then in white, we cut a hole in its upper part through which we can pass plugs for our pump and our pipes. That's all the tank needs.

For this to work, however, we need to connect it to a pipe. Connect the hose to the hose and pass it through the bucket. You can use glue, tape or another preferred method to hold the tube in place and feed the plants. One effective way is to create a loop inside the bucket, insert many small holes in the bucket, and then connect this pipe to the main pipe. In this way, the water would flow through the main pipe, which is connected to the inner pipe of the blade, and act as a mini sprinkler system. This way the water flows over the bucket and is not limited to one area.

After installing the supply pipe, we need to fix the delivery pipe. It is so easy to connect our hose to the hole we use and bring it back to the tank. It is important that the bucket is well above the tank so that gravity can do its job.

To avoid melting our plants, it is important to have a digital clock and plug it in so as not to constantly pump water. You want to get a clock that we can use to set many different times, not just once, because our system has to be turned on and off several times a day, not just once. We need to do this to make sure our plants are getting the right amount of nutrients.

How to set up a single cup drip system. If you want to extend the system, it's really very simple. Suppose you want to create four compartments instead of just one. They take these buckets and give them their holes and their paint. The main difference between starting a single bucket set and starting a four bucket set is the hose. Instead of running a pipe from our tank to the bucket, we rather use T-pieces.

Remove the hose that drains from the tank and connect it to the T-piece. This gives you a tube that looks like the T-curve we see on the street. Instead of being a single tube with one end, you now have two tubes with their own ends. This would allow us to use the two-compartment configuration. In this example, however, we have chosen the four-compartment configuration. This means that we have to take each of these lamps and restart them at the tee. Now, each side is divided into two parts and we have four ends, one for each of our buckets, and we have quadrupled the size of our harvest.

When the whole building is in place, all we have to do is pack our buckets. Some stones at the bottom of each bucket k of aid can weigh them, but this is not essential. This is more of an Precautions of the exception, although it is recommended. And here you have your own hydroponic drip system.

Humidity management system

As we saw above, vacuuming is actually the easiest system to get started. It is also one of the easiest systems to build because it requires very little technical skill. All we need to get started is a growing tray, reservoir, and wick.

Penetration is simply the use of material that can enter the culture bowl from our tank. It can be a rope, a felt, a string; Any material readily available for moisture management works.

We first create our tank and fill it with the nutrient solution of our choice, which of course depends on what we are growing (more information on nutrient solutions can be found in Chapter 4). We will repaint the tank in black and then cover it with white paint to avoid algae support or excessive heating. Then we cut or drill very small holes in the tank cap through which we drill our wicks.

Our complimentary trays are filled with a medium particularly adapted to the evacuation of humidity, such as perlite or coconut. But before filling them, let's start by cutting or drilling small holes in the bottom of the tray, as we did with the tank cap. They will be roughly the same size because this is how the wick provides plants with nutrients.

After all, our wicks are almost completely submerged in water. This does not necessarily mean that they are touching the bottom of the tank, but they are definitely approaching. They are then fed and nestled in a tank so that they can grow very close to the plants. You can use more than one wick per plant, depending on the specific needs of the plant in terms of water and nutrients.

When it comes to configuration, it really is. We put our plants on a growing tray and watch how they grow. However, a few tips and tricks make a more efficient transfer system more efficient. We can consider aerating the water with an air pump so that our plants get more oxygen as this helps them grow faster. Another thing we want to consider is to bring the culture tank of the tank with a system of moisture transfer with a system of drip. This is because in this system, no nutrient is pumped into our plants, but that it must be based on a so-called capillary action (i.e. percolation). With our wicks, shorter resources can be secured more easily. The distance between our wicks and the culture plate is one way. Second, you need to make sure that the water level in our tank is high, as this also shortens the distance.

This system is also not suitable for plants that require a lot of water and nutrients since nutrient drainage is a slow process. However, herbs and lettuce can grow wonderful plants in a moisture management system, making it easy to introduce the concept of hydroponics to someone unfamiliar with the subject. They even do great projects to encourage children to practice hydroponics and gardening!

Culture Deep Sea

Despite the fact that the drainage system is the easiest hydroponic system to use in the garden, deep water cultivation is almost as easy to install. For our explanation, we will create a culture in deep water. This means that we conceive as if we are growing a medium plant. This system can be adapted to many small factories. However, if we want to multiply, we must first change our culture to a larger container.

Since deep water is used in deep-sea culture (after all, by name), we will be using a 5 gallon bucket because of the depth we have. Although some people call each floating plant system a deep water system, we actually need ten inches of water to be considered deep. We could grow a small plant in a small crop and give it the equivalent of a deep water crop, but you still wouldn't call it that.

The first thing that we are going to surprise is to paint the bucket in black then in white. We will also cut a small hole under the cover for the hose of our air pump so that we can provide oxygen water. With these two steps, we can put our spoons aside.

Since growing in deep water submerges the roots of the plant in water, we need to design the system so that our plants can bathe. For this we can buy a so-called basket of plants. This basket looks like a typical flowerpot, but instead has many holes in the bottom half. Alternatively, we can take the pot and then cut, drill or weld holes in it. It will be our culture platform.

We fill our growing bowl with the desired growing medium and the plant we want to grow, but first we have to integrate it into the system. To do this, we drilled a hole in the lid of our 5-gallon bucket. At this point it is better to cut a small hole and enlarge it properly rather than starting from a large hole. This is because it is much easier to enlarge the hole than to lock it. If we make our hole too big, our tray just falls into the bucket and we have to get another lid and try again. Our goal is that the bottom half of the pot fits into the hole and is held on the lid of the bucket at the edge of the pot.

Before that, we drilled a hole in the bucket directly under the cover of our air pump. The reason we didn't cut it on the lid itself is that we don't want to mess with the wires when we open our system to check the pH and make sure all the nutrients are balanced. When we open our system, we only need to remove the lid and therefore the jar.

Everything should be in place now. We fill the bucket with our water and lift it to cover three quarters of the hanging pot. We can first test it on clear water, then mark the desired water level on our buckets so that we can look further more easily. Mix the medium, fill the pot with the desired medium and add the plant or seeds.

It will take about a week for the roots of the plant to protrude from the holes we drilled in our pot. It is therefore important to ensure that the water level is high enough for our plants to get the moisture they need. When the roots start to collapse, the water level no longer matters.

In addition, here you are, you just created a culture on the high seas for your plants. Although you can grow small or medium plants in this same crop, you will probably want to grow multiple plants. But as you have seen, it should not take much time.

CHAPTER 3

A CYCLE OF EXPLOITATION

After setting up the hydroponic system, we take some time to see how it works. This means that we are looking at the different types of growth media available to us to find out which are the best for each type of configuration. We will also look at how we plant our hydroponic gardens, how we light them and what we do when it comes to pruning.

Growing substrates

Regarding the support we use in our culture bowls, we have a large choice. First, it can be a little intimidating if you are not sure which remedy is right for you and which gardening you are looking for. It is important to choose a support that will work with the plants you want to plant. This means that we have to consider things like water retention and pH balance.

Before examining the media ourselves, a quick word on the requirements of the different systems. The way each system is configured and works say a lot about the type of substrate that grows best. For example, a drip system works best when you use growth media that are not too wet. The wicking system, on the other hand, likes a substrate that easily absorbs and retains water and moisture. While nutrient film systems want to avoid slightly saturated substrates, the drainage and drainage, system wants good drainage and a non-floating substrate. Taking into account the mechanics of the selected system is the first step in deciding on a growing substrate.

Coco Coir

Coconut-coconut is an inert, organic growth medium and is made from serrated and ground coconut shells. In terms of pH, coconut is almost neutral. Coco Coir retains water, but also allows the right amount of oxygen to penetrate, which helps the roots. This medium is mainly used in container cultures or in passive type hydroponic systems such as permeation. Because it can clog pumps and wastewater, it is not a good choice for more active systems like drainage and flow.

Gravel

Gravel does not absorb or store moisture. Instead, the gravel anchors the roots of the plant. For this reason, gravel works best in a system that does not require much retention, such as B. a drip system or a nutritional film technology system. Any system that keeps plant roots in constant contact with water can use gravel well.

In some configurations, such as the cup-based drip system shown above, gravel is used as the bottom layer in the pot. This allows for better drainage since water has flowed through any medium that forms the top layer to find gravel that does not stop at all. It is also used to increase the weight of the bottom of the tray, preventing wind leaks or other objects.

If you are using gravel, you must wash it thoroughly before using it in the system. If you want to reuse gravel, wash it again. We do this to avoid salt or bacteria in the scope of hydroponics and problems such as burnt roots, high toxicity and as a cause. Frayed gravel can also damage the roots. It is best to use smooth gravel to avoid this.

Nacre

Perlite improves drainage and ventilation when mixed with another medium such as coconut. Since we use a mixture of nutrients, not just clean water, we have to worry about the formation of nutrients. The nutrients in our solutions can be absorbed by the nutrient solution and lead to an accumulation of toxicity, which threatens to kill our plants. No gardener wants it. The additional drainage provided by perlite prevents this material from accumulating and ensures that our plant's root system receives the oxygen it needs to grow. Perlite comes in different types, from small to medium to thick. The rest of your soil determines the type you need. Perlite does should never take more than one third of your mix, but if you use too much, it will float and floating perlite no advantage at first.

Vermiculite

Vermiculite actually looks like perlite. There are three different types, from thin to medium to thick. Another change in the soil and pot mixture is vermiculite, which is generated by the expansion of mica by heat. This means that the vermiculite is mixed with another growth medium for best results.

Vermiculite acts like an inverted perlite. While perlite helped drain our nutrient solution, vermiculite helps our nutrient to retain water. For this reason, vermiculite can often be mixed with perlite for use in passive hydroponic systems such as permeation systems.

Rockwool

Rock wool, one of the most popular growth media, is made by heating and spinning a particular silica-based rock made of cotton candy material. This creates a durable material with an ideal water-to-oxygen ratio that the roots of our plants love. It is also mainly at neutral pH, which is always a plus.

It can be found in many different shapes and sizes, the most common being the shape of a cube. These dice are great for starting seeds (which we'll cover in more detail shortly). These small cubes are often used to start plant growth before moving to another growth medium.

Due to its versatility, Rockwool can be used to plant plants before they are transferred to another medium for deep-water crops or film wrap systems. It can also be used in drip and drainage systems as well as in drainage systems without the need for a transmission.

Mix the growth medium

When it comes to the best substrate, it depends on the job you want to deal with. Once you have an idea of what you need, you can mix it all up. Many different models on the market offer premixed growth media. This can be a great way to save time and get what you need right away.

However, some of us are a little more specific and we want to get our hands dirty in this part of the process. Mixing your own growth medium can be a great way to make sure it is 100% what you want it to be. However, this can be a bit difficult if you are new to hydroponics and do not know which combination of measures is best. Part of getting started with something new, and hydroponic gardening is nothing else, is that you have to accept uncomfortable moments and accept that you will learn from your mistakes.

Let us look at an example of a mixture of what Upstartfarmers.com presented in the discussion of ungrounded pots. They offer a mixed formula of one-component coconut or peat, one-part perlite or wormwood, and two-part compost. Although the systems we have examined do not focus on compost, but on the delivery of nutrients through the solution in our tank, this shows us a simple mix. Note that perlite or vermiculite does not exceed 33% (or 1/3) of the total mixture.

Seedling

When it comes to introducing plants into our hydroponic system, we have two options. We can go to the store and buy a seedling, which we can then transplant into our system. Alternatively, we can buy seeds and grow plants ourselves. In this section, we will look at this last option to see how we can turn seeds into wonderful plants in our hydroponic gardens. However, this means that we will also look at the first option, because when our seeds are ready to be transferred to our hydroponic configurations, we will replant them in cuttings.

Growing a plant from seeds is very satisfying. They start with small grains and can still grow into such large, succulent plants. It is a wonderful feeling to know that you are responsible for it. However, growing from seeds has more benefits than just the feeling we have.

Buying seeds gives you many options for growing the plants you want. Not all seeds will take, but enough is enough to easily get a ton of seedlings at the same price as you would get a seedling. This makes it an inexpensive solution that looks really incredible. Buying seeds also gives you more control over what you grow, as you are not limited to just the plants the company had available at the start of the research. That means you can choose what to grow, and it can be rare and esoteric plants, or just lettuce and herbs. The choice is yours.

If you are growing seeds directly in the hydroponic system you want to use, you don't have to worry about how to replant the green for the new system. This can be a way to avoid injury to plants or damage to roots. Planting in the system can also be a way to introduce diseases or pests into the garden, and we want to avoid this if possible.

If we decide to start with seeds, it costs us a bit in advance because we have to do a few things to grow. However, these costs are mainly at the start. If you have already started with seeds, you can expect to save money on your next visit. The good news is that you don't really have to do without buying highly specialized equipment or materials to grow seeds. All the materials collected can be used in other phases of the process.

Assuming you have harvested seeds, what do you need to start them in your hydroponic garden? The first thing we need is a culture tray. This may be what we founded earlier, or we can use the dome to create a miniature greenhouse. Don't worry, if you don't have one that fits this description, this is just one way to help our seeds. We can use any available culture container.

We want to make sure that we place the growing tray in such a way as to create good light - if the plants are of the type that likes light very much. We also want to make sure the tray receives the right amount of heat. If you receive a heating pad or keep it in a warm place, this will ensure that germination begins.

After configuring the compartment, you want to get some first plugins. These are small compact masses of solid growth medium that are used specifically for the growth of our seeds. They generally consist of composted pine and peat or other organic substances. We can buy or manufacture them because they are essentially small cubes of material with a small hole in which we can put our seeds.

Open the cap and put seeds in it. We will make some if one of the seeds refuses to take. With repeated harvests, we can always eliminate the weaker plant so that the stronger one can grow even better. After throwing the seeds into the hole, pluck a small piece of cork and use it to block the hole. They do this to prevent the seeds from drying out or being thrown out of the cork.

You need about a centimeter of nutrient solution in the growth bowl, although this centimeter should be half the usual size. Place the accessories in the compartment. You can expect sprouts to appear within four to five days of planting. Make sure to constantly monitor the water level and add more nutrients as the water level drops.

This is how you grow from seeds. If you put it now on the main growing tray, you don't have to worry about replanting it later, and you can just let it grow and look at it like any other plant in the garden. If you but in a specially designed germinator run leave, you must transplant them into your system.

When your seedlings start to grow, you can stop worrying about having the strength of the nutrient solution and start with a regular mixture of starch solution. If you see the roots of the cuttings sticking out of the bottom of the starter plug, it is a sign that you can now start replanting them. This can take two to four weeks; It all depends on the plants you grow.

Once the cuttings are finished, take them and carefully transfer them to your hydroponic set. To do this, take a seedling and an ankle together. You want to open a place in the garden, carefully place the cube and seedlings at this point, then carefully cover with the selected substrate. After that, you need to water the plant from above for a few days so that its root system develops and searches for water and nutrients naturally.

And that's all! Now you have grown your own plant, from seeds to cuttings, to transplantation and the natural development of the root system. By working with the seeds in this way, we can take more control over what we grow and make sure we don't bring any problems to our garden that are found in the plants available in the store.

Lighting

Solar energy cannot be replaced in lighting. There is a reason why spring and summer are such beautiful green seasons. The sun is absolutely the most powerful light source available for plants.

However, we won't use it here anyway. Instead, we will use artificial light in order to have total control over it. In addition, many of us are interested in hydroponics because we do not have access to outdoor spaces where you can create a garden. If you live in an apartment, you are probably reading this because it gives you the opportunity to grow your own food without leaving your house. If you can configure a hydroponic garden to use natural sunlight, that's perfect! But if you can't, you have to look at the artificial light and we will investigate.

There are tons of tons of lighting options available. So much so that it can be really overwhelming if you are new to the subject. What size of light do you want? What spectrum of colors should it play? Damn, how much light is the right amount? It can be intimidating. But don't worry, it sounds a lot easier than all of these options.

We can use the sun to do this depending on the amount of light. If we plant outdoors, we can expect to need about five hours of direct sunlight and another ten indirect rays of sunlight. That means five hours of sunbathing and ten hours outside, but in the shade. With this system, we can adapt our artificial lighting accordingly. With artificial light, we need to give our hydroponic garden about fourteen hours of bright light and ten hours of darkness. If you make this system every day, the natural cycle of solar lighting is imitated. Don't save in the dark. You may think that more light means faster growth, but plants are like us because they need to rest and metabolize the nutrients they receive.

Some plants need more light, others less. You can think of the fourteen to ten system as a general. This system works well for most plants and can certainly be a successful path to take for the garden. However, you should definitely be aware of the lighting requirements of your plants.

Plants with a long day are those that want up to eighteen hours of sunshine a day. These mimic the longer cycle of the day that occurs during the summer season. Examples of day plants are lettuce, potatoes, spinach and beets. Because they like more light, you don't want to mix long-day plants with short-day plants in the same bowl. If so, expect a lighting cycle that meets both long and short requirements.

There are also more neutral plants. These plants are generally flexible and can work with more or less light when needed. Eggplants and corn are examples of this type of plant. Neutral day plants can be mixed with short or long day plants and grow as well.

Since you want to imitate the sun, it is best to get a timer to light a hydroponic garden. If you have already installed the drainage and drainage system, you probably have time to make sure that your nutrient solution can drain before washing it again. We use the same type of timer, but instead of being configured for the pump, we set it on our lights. The duration of setting the timer depends on what you grow and your lighting needs, as explained above.

As for the lights themselves, we have to move on to the discussion of light bulbs. The most popular hydroponic bulb generally has between 400 and 600 watts and has a type known as high intensity discharge. These lamps are usually enclosed in glass (with gas and metallic salts thrown into the mixture) and generate light by sending electricity between two electrodes inside. The gas helps the bulb create an arc and the metal salts evaporate and produce a white light. They are available in two versions: high pressure sodium and metal halide lamps.

The metal halide lamp is a versatile light that most vegetables will love. If you have to choose between metal halides or high-pressure sodium lamps, metal halide is the best choice. They are generally expensive and cost over $ 150 for a 400-watt bulb. However, they must be replaced every two years, although they may reduce effectiveness sooner.

High-pressure sodium bulbs are best suited for the flowering of our plants. They are even more expensive than metal halide lamps, but are usually extended twice. However, they lose power just like metal halide lamps.

If we want to increase the efficiency of our bulbs, we can use a headlight cover. It is a reflective housing that surrounds the bulb and increases its efficiency by reflecting the light around it. As a result, light hits our plants from different angles so that we can expand more effectively in our garden. It is also used to extract a little more heat from incandescent lamps, since the light rays now intersect and form a denser section, thereby transferring more heat and power.

So regarding lighting and you can only get one bulb, go out and get the metal halide lamp and the reflector cover. Get a retarder and adapt it to the needs of your plants. When you buy plants, you usually get a label with information about the light requirements of the plant or seeds. After that and by setting the appropriate timer, make sure your plants are getting as lighter as they need.

Cut

The last step in the operating cycle of our hydroponic gardens is pruning. When the plants are frec, nature plays the role of gardener and mower. These plants can last for many years and sometimes even a lifetime without pruning or pruning. As soon as you bring the plants home, in a hydroponic kit or in a greenhouse, people immediately grab a pruner. If we look at the image of gardening we have in our heads, we see that films and television have repeatedly told us that we want to prune our plants. The characters always do that!

But the truth is that this. Improper pruning puts unnecessary pressure on our plants and can seriously damage them and even lead to disease or infection. Indeed, every time we prune our plants, we open the wound. We have cut the branch; we have just opened our factories. Where the hand was figurative, there is only the stump. When you think about the human body, you can understand why things can go wrong. We must show the body of our plants the same respect that we would show to others. This means that when you move to trim, you must make sure to sterilize the cutting instrument between each cut. This can be done simply by mixing four parts of water with one part of bleach and immersing the scissors in the solution before each cut.

If pruning our plants can be so dangerous, why did we choose them? There are actually several reasons. One of them is that we want to control the overall size of our factories. If we grow indoors, we can prune our plants to prevent them from reaching and disrupting walking or television, etc. This is the same reason why we cut branches when they get too close to power lines. We can also prune our plants to improve their health and flowering quality. If a particular piece of the plant is dead and rotten, we need to remove it to improve the health of the plant. We may also want to remove the parts that have not flowered properly so that the healthy flowering parts have more space to breathe and expand. It also prevents the system from consuming energy to repair damaged parts and can instead use this energy for cultivation.

One of the reasons why you should not cut the plants is to increase the overall yield. Pruning does not help our plants in this way. Instead of pruning to gain weight, we must prune to promote better health.

When we have decided where to cut, we know that we need a solution to sterilize our scissors. Another way to prevent disease during the cutting process is to pinch the tips of the plant where the cut was made. This will help the extremities to heal faster. It's a bit like sewing an arm injury. They want to keep the goals together so that treatment is promoted and the time required for treatment is reduced. Because pruning plants is so stressful and healing requires energy, you should only prune when necessary, and you should not just prune unwittingly. It is best to prune a little, wait for the plant to heal, and then prune a little more than doing it all at once.

If the reason for pruning a plant is that it grows too high in your home, you need to do something called "replenishment." When we prune in this way, we cut off the top of the main stem of the plant. When we make the cut, we will press it for each of our cuts. However, if you squeeze the top of the main stem after cutting, the plant releases flowering hormones, which forces the plant to focus on lateral growth rather than upward. The same technique can then be applied to these lateral branches to have the opposite effect when they grow back. In this way, we can control the growth patterns of our plants. Irrigation also has a strange effect when gardeners notice that the watered plants generally produce more berries. Meanwhile, plants that have not been sprinkled generally produce less fruit but are large.

If you cut damaged and dying leaves, you should only remove leaves that are more than half damaged. These leave no longer energize plants and deprive some of them to care for them. There is a misconception that the leaves of the plant if they are yellow should immediately be removed. Changing the yellow leaves, however, is the way the plant tries to tell you that something is wrong. This usually means that the plant is under a lot of stress. This can mean that not getting the necessary nutrients, and light, and can even cause the COG cable installation to have a problem with insects. When your plant's leaves turn yellow, watch what the plant is trying to tell you before you start cutting. If you solve the problem, you will often find that the leaves become greener and healthier again.

So when it's time to prune the plants, be sure to sterilize your instruments, consider how much stress you are putting on the plant, and only make cuts that are strictly necessary. We want to grow healthy and fertile plants, which means respecting the body of your plants as you respect yours.

CHAPTER 4

BEST PLANTS FOR GARDEN AND HYDROPONIC NUTRITION

We know what the hydroponic garden layouts are, how we make them, and what type of operational cycle we can expect. In this chapter, we will examine the different plants available for cultivation. We will take a look at each plant to find out how it grows best in our hydroponic configurations. From now on, we will take care of the nutrition that our plants need.

Vegetable

When it comes to vegetables, there are many options to choose from. We will examine a handful of them but first, examine the general principles.

First, there are vegetables that grow underground. These are vegetables like onions, carrots, and potatoes. These plants can still be grown in a hydroponic system, but require additional work compared to plants that grow above the surface, such as lettuce, cabbage, and beans. This means that these underground installations require slightly more advanced skills and you may want to gain some experience with the hydroponic system before attempting to use them.

The second rule is that we must avoid plants like corn, zucchini and anything that is based on the cultivation of many vines. These types of plants take up a lot of space and are simply not very practical plants for hydroponic systems. Instead of focusing on the type of installation that is not practical, we can make better use of our space and systems.

Beans

There are many types of beans, from green beans to green beans, lima beans to pinto beans. Depending on the type of beans you are planting, you can add a grid to your set. Beans offer a wide range of ingredients and are a great addition to any meal. In terms of temperature, beans prefer a warm place. They also prefer a pH of around 6.0.

If you grow beans from seeds, you can expect them to grow for three to eight days. From there, you can expect six to eight weeks before harvest. After the start of the harvest, the harvest can be continued for three or four months.

Cucumbers

As with beans, there are several options when it comes to the type of cucumber we can grow. There are thick-skinned American slicers, smooth-skinned Lebanese cucumbers, and seedless European cucumbers. So great a variety and the best news is that they all grow quite well in a hydroponic configuration. Where beans prefer warm temperature, cucumbers prefer hot smoothing. They like to go further than the heat. They also prefer a pH between 5.5 and 6.0

Cucumbers don't start to germinate until three to ten days. Harvest preparation takes eight to ten weeks. When picking cucumbers, make sure the cucumbers are dark green in color and hard when you catch them. Since each cucumber grows at a different rate, you can expect the harvest to take a while because you don't want to harvest it until it's finished.

Kale

Kale is a delicious and nutritious vegetable suitable for every meal. Kale has so many health benefits that it is often considered food. Kale actually prefers a slightly lower temperature; grows best in the cold to the hot range. Like cucumber, kale prefers a pH of 5.5 to 6.0.

The germ seeds only last four to seven days. However, the harvest takes nine to eleven weeks. Kale grows a little longer than beans or cucumbers but can be harvested so that it continues to grow. If you only collect 30% kale at one time, you can grow back quickly.

Salad

It is great because salads can be made with lettuce, sandwiches and burgers have a little texture and taste, and it's just a versatile and versatile vegetable that you can have in the kitchen.

Lettuce cultivation offers many varieties. Although lettuce prefers a low temperature and a low pH between 6.0 and 7.0, it works in any hydroponic system you create. For this reason, lettuce is excellent input for hydroponics. Lettuce germination takes only a few days, but the harvest time depends on the type of salad you have chosen. For example, curly lettuce takes only 45 to 50 days to harvest. Romaine lettuce can last up to eighty-five days.

Paprika

Like tomatoes, paprika is technically a fruit, but it is so closely linked to vegetable dishes and plants that many people consider them vegetables. For this reason, we will cover both peppers and tomatoes in this chapter. Peppers have many similarities to tomatoes in their growth preferences. Peppers like pH values between 5.5 and 6.0 and temperatures from hot to hot ß.

You can start peppers from seeds or cuttings. The peppers ripen in about two to three months. When you think of the pepper to grow, you should know that jalapeno; habanero, Mazurek, Fellini, Nairobi and cubic peppers are great for hydroponics.

Radish

Like lettuce, radishes are one of the easiest plants to grow, whether in a traditional vegetable garden or in a hydroponic configuration. As suggested in the last chapter, radishes are best grown from seeds rather than cuttings, and it only takes three to seven days to start planting. Radishes grow well with lettuce because of both plants like cool temperatures and pH values between 6.0 and 7.0.

The great thing about radishes is that, unlike most plants, they do not need light. This means that if the cost of getting the light right outside the door is too high, radishes provide a way to test hydroponics in the garden before dropping the money. The crazy thing is that radishes can grow very quickly and are sometimes ready to be harvested in a month!

Spinach

Spinach is another plant that grows well in combination with lettuce and radishes. Spinach has low temperatures and a pH between 6.0 and 7.0, so it fits perfectly. You need something lighter than radish, but it doesn't take much.

Tomatoes

Okay, okay, we all know that tomatoes are technically fruits. But let's take a look here because with the rest of the vegetables in this section, add the tomatoes and you have a great salad! Tomatoes grow best in a warm environment, and you need to put a rack on the grow tray. They also like the pH between 5.5 and 6.5.

Tomatoes are different; From the traditional ones, we see here to the little cherry tomatoes that create delicious snacks. Germination can be expected between five and ten days and it takes a month or two before seeing the fruit. You can expect fifty to a hundred days to prepare the harvest, and the size and color of the tomatoes can be determined.

Fruits

Nothing tastes as sweet as the fruit you have grown yourself. Hydroponic gardening is a great way to grow fruit in the comfort of your home. As with vegetables, there are many options, but we will focus on the ones that grow best.

Blueberries

Perfect for snacks, baking, and even adding vitamins to your morning meal. Blueberries are a fantastic crop. However, it can be difficult to germinate berries from seeds. It is therefore recommended to replant berry plants instead. Berries are one of the slowest plants that bear fruit, and even producing them for up to a year can take up to over a year. They like it at pH 4.5 to 6.0 in a warm climate.

Strawberries

The most popular fruits of hydroponics are strawberries grown in smaller personal hydroponic configurations and in larger cash crops. Strawberries prefer a warm temperature and pH 6.0 and grow best in the nutrient film system.

Blueberries and strawberries together are great fruit crops that they can produce for several years if you give them the time to grow.

Herbs

Herbs are a great addition to any hydroponic package. Indeed, it has been proven that hydroponic herbs contain 20 to 40% more aromatic oils than herbs grown in a traditional garden. That means you get more hydroponic herbs with less consumption.

The best system for growing weeds is drainage and drainage. Hydroponic herb gardens have become the norm worldwide due to their effectiveness. Right now, there are even restaurants that grow their own hydroponic herb gardens, as this is the most effective way to get fresh herbs of incredible quality.

Basil is the most popular herb, and basil accounts for around 50% of the herb market in Europe. Basil and mint like a warm environment and a pH between 5.5 and 6.5. Likewise, chives prefer a hot to hot temperature and the pH is around 6.0. This means that if you pay attention to temperature and pH, you can grow these three wonderful herbs in the same hydroponic configuration.

An herb garden is a great way to start hydroponics. They can stay harvested for an incredibly long time; they taste better than herbs grown in the ground and complement each meal perfectly. In addition, herb gardens are generally smaller than vegetable gardens or orchards, so a hydroponic herb garden takes up less space and can save on preparation costs.

Hydroponic Nutrition

In this section, we will look at the nutrient solution we use to fill our tanks and provide our plants with what they need to grow and stay strong. In order to understand this important component of our hydroponic systems, we will study macro and micronutrients, how important it is to test the needs of our plants and how we mix our own solution so that the pH and electrical conductivity are in the right balance

What is a nutritional solution?

When we talk about the nutrients we use in our tanks, we are talking about properly dosed liquid fertilizer. Although there are many trading options on the market today, we will look at how to mix ours. In this way, even if we choose the option purchased in store, we know how to optimally control the nutrition of our hydroponic garden.

When it comes to plant growth, 16 elements combine the nutrients we use, our water and our oxygen in the air. The nutrient solution replaces the nutrients in the soil by combining them in our water.

It is important to know what nutrients our plants expect because they differ from each other. There are more plants in the world than we can describe in a book. It is therefore important to learn how to find this information on your own. The best way to do this is to open Google and search for "plant name + hydroponic nutritional requirements". If you were growing tomatoes, it would look like "the hydroponic nutritional requirements of tomatoes". If you look at the search results, you will find that almost all of the headings "Requirements for Tomato Fertilizers" or "Nutrition for Tomato Plants" and "What nutrients do tomato plants need?" Each of these websites provides the information you need. I recommend that you visit multiple websites, not just one, to see if your needs change or if your website provides more detailed information.

Basic macro-elements

When we talk about essential macronutrients, we mean the nutrients that our plants need in large quantities. Macronutrients are fats, proteins, and carbohydrates for humans. Although plants retain these ingredients, it's more about how they produce them and how they handle them. When it comes to the nutrients they are looking for, our plants love nitrogen, phosphorus, and potassium. We want to make sure that we have the right proportions of these big three so that our plants can stay healthy, produce more abundant crops, and continue to grow.

Nitrogen

Nitrogen, which is found in amino acids, chlorophyll and nucleic acids, is an element made up of enzymes and proteins. While humans love protein in its pure form, plants love it when it passes nitrogen. If your plants are not getting enough nitrogen, they will have a protein content of more weak. On the other hand, too much nitrogen leads to darker leaves and contributes to the vegetative growth of plants.

We want to make sure that our plants have an adequate nitrogen balance, as this ensures that our plants are stronger, use their own carbohydrates better, stay healthier and produce more protein.

Phosphorus

Phosphorus is really the main element of the RNA, DNA and ATP systems of our plants. This is scientific terminology, which says that phosphorus is very important for our plants. A lack of phosphorus can make our plants mature longer. That, but poor plant and root growth can not only lead to lower yields and see how the fruits of the plants fall before they ripen. Likewise, too much phosphorus can cause a lack of zinc (a micronutrient) in our plants.

Our plants want enough phosphorus to better use photosynthesis. It also helps our plants to control cell division and regulate how they use starch and sugar.

Potassium

Potassium is the last of our three main macronutrients and a little less important than nitrogen and phosphorus. This should not be justified by ignoring the level of potassium in our nutrient solutions. If our plants do not get enough potassium, there is a risk that they will have weaker stems and affect performance. If we have too much potassium, we also interfere with the absorption of magnesium by our plants.

When our plants get the right amount of potassium, we make sure they use water from our tanks as much as possible. Potassium also helps plants resist disease, metabolize their nutrients and even regulate excess water.

Trace elements

When we talk about micronutrients, we mean seven different nutrients that our plants love. These are boron, chlorine, copper, iron, manganese, molybdenum and zinc. Together, these micronutrients are not as important as our macronutrients, but they are still very important.

Usually, gardeners add micronutrients only when their plants show signs of a certain deficiency. But before you start adding traces of nutrients to your mix, make sure you that the problem is the same nutrients. For example, a deficiency can be caused by parasites or a low pH. If we add micronutrients to our mixtures and the problem has nothing to do with micronutrients, there is a risk that our plants will be damaged. For this reason, you should first consider all possible causes and exclude as many as possible before looking for micronutrients.

Mix your own solution

The first thing we need to do to mix our own solution is to know exactly what our factories need. As we did above, in the section "What is a nutritional solution?" With the information you found in this section, you can find out exactly what your plants want. We will use this information here to supplement the specifics of this approach.

Before we start mixing our solution, we must first buy materials. We have to lift a few buckets. We need a bucket for each part of the solution. Three buckets seem to be a good number because they allow us to confront the system they call A, B, Bloom. Some systems only need two compartments because mixing only involves two stages. You also want to buy a digital scale that can fall to hundredths of a gram. And of course we have to buy nutritious salts which will be our solutions. These are salts that decay in water and give us the macro elements we need. You can buy them at any hydroponic garden store. Amazon.com offers both pre-mixed nutrient solutions and raw nutrients that you need to mix.

You should also make sure you have clean measuring cups and rubber gloves to keep you safe. You want to fill the buckets with the right amount of water needed for each part of the solution. It depends on the type of mixture your specific plants need for a custom amount to be available. We have to make sure our water is clean. It is always best to use a filter system to remove contaminants that may be present in the water.

With the scale, you weigh the right amount of nutritious salt. After reaching this amount, slowly pour the salt into the first bucket of water. Do this slowly to avoid splashing water and losing some of the solution in this process. You should see the salts begin to dissolve almost immediately after touching the water. After finishing the first, measure the salts for the second part of the solution. Repeat until all parts of the solution are mixed in your own buckets . You can put the lids on and shake them to make sure there is no heap of undissolved nutrients.

After making our blend (or blends), we need to check the pH. We know that most plants prefer something between 5.5 and 6.5. Water is a neutral medium, which means that it has a pH of 7 tester to prepare the pH level and preparation to work. You want to dilute a lower pH solution, so mix a few drops in a gallon of water. This should give you a solution similar to 2.0. The nutrients you use increase the pH of your water. So you should start at 2.0 and increase as you mix. Then slowly add this diluted mixture to your nutrient solution. Make sure to add it slowly and stop checking the pH frequently.

After balancing the pH, check the electrical conductivity of the mixture. To do this, you need an EC electronic measuring device. Electrical conductivity allows us to accurately read the balance of nutrients and the pH value. Since we mixed our own nutrient solution, we had to use mineral salts to get the nutrients we wanted. We can calculate the number of nutrients in the solution by electrical conductivity. Most plants want an EC between 1.5 and 2.5, so this can be a great way to verify that we have the right mix before giving it to our plants.

If we get below 1.5, it means we do not have enough nutrients in our solution, so we need to add more, in order to increase them. If it is too high, we risk exposing our plants to hot nutrients. Burning food refers to the physical signs that our plants are getting too many nutrients. Burning leaves is an obvious symptom of burns. Another common burn symptom is root burns. We want to grow healthy plants, so we should not overfeed them with too many nutrients.

After checking if your EC value meets your needs, you have successfully mixed your own nutrient solution. While the specifics depend on the plants you choose to grow, this overview should show that it's really not all that difficult to create your own solutions and keep control of our hydroponic systems and the health of our plants.

CHAPTER 5

MAINTAINING YOUR HYDROPONIC GARDEN

At this point, we have developed our hydroponic systems, selected the plants we want to grow and mixed some of the nutrient solution together to provide them with all the macronutrients they may need. So far, you can safely call yourself a hydroponic gardener! But the work is not yet finished. Now that you have your plan and you are growing plants; you must be vigilant when maintaining your hydroponic garden.

This chapter contains many tools that you can use to keep your garden running smoothly. To this end, we will examine how we decontaminate our culture space and how we sterilize it. These two words are often used interchangeably, but in fact they are two different levels. Next, we'll look at how to keep our tanks in good condition, read general troubleshooting tips, and show how our factories tell us they need help. Due to the importance of the information in this section, we will close these sections with a brief summary of what you need to do in your garden.

Decontamination

When it comes to decontaminating our hydroponic gardens, we think of giving our garden a deep cleanliness. The cleanliness of our gardens is just as important as replacing a burnt out bulb or the right balance of our nutrients. Proper disinfection kills and eliminates most of the microorganisms that can cause damage. The first step in the disinfection you want to do is to make sure that any spilled material, excess water or draining plants are removed immediately. You can buy a wet and dry vacuum cleaner that can be used to remove spilled liquids. Although this is a useful tool, you can also do it manually. You want to make sure to spill it quickly and clean it completely, because extra moisture on the floor can increase the humidity in the room. Increasing humidity increases the risk of mold entering our systems. There is also a risk of decay of our plants, which is the plant's worst nightmare. In addition, leaks can damage the floor, which can result in the payment of repairs.

Whenever you enter a room where you are operating a hydroponic garden, you will want to look for dead plants that you can find. Every day you should spend time checking for dead leaves and other dead plant material.

It is also extremely tempting for various pests (we will see how to manage them in the next chapter). Make sure to always remove old roots and plants when harvesting, rather than storing them for later.

When it comes to planting rot problems, many gardeners never notice that the problem is due to the cleanliness of the growing area. In the last chapter, we found that we want to make sure that the problem with our plants is nothing else before we start adding micronutrients to our solutions. It is one of those situations in which people draw conclusions. One of the first things we need to check is that we have kept the garden room clean.

If your hydroponic configuration uses an inlet filter, you should check and clean it at least once a week. These filters prevent dust, worms, and mold from entering our culture bowls. Routine cleaning of the inlet filter ensures maximum airflow through the system. It is also a way to prevent pests that try to enter your garden quickly. If you find the pest on the inlet filter, you can quickly prevent spoilage and damage to the garden.

Every few months, you should also remove the bulbs from your lamps and wipe them dry. You should also do this with each glass you have, for example, B. if you are using a reflector with light. For example, if you plan it every three months, you can plan it in advance and make sure you don't overlook this cleaning. Harvesting can also be a good time to access this cleaning, as we generally open up more space when we collect our plants and facilitate access to our equipment. You can use a glass cleaner or isopropyl alcohol to clean this glass. We want to follow this cleaning because dirt can accumulate on our glasses and lamps and this can reduce the light flux that we can provide to our plants.

You should also disinfect you are grow room devices as often as you wash the glass. This means that we are wiping our pumps, hoses, etc. You even want to wipe the outside of the grass catcher and tank. If you have devices that have exposed the circuit, you must use a few cans of compressed air so that you can clean them without damaging the electronics.

Conclusion: Remove spilled substances as soon as they occur. Check for dead plant material once a day. Check the inlet filters weekly. Every few months, you must enter and clean the glass and the bulbs used in the lighting configuration. When cleaning the glass, you should also use compressed air on everything you use for quick cleaning of anything with exposed circuits.

Sterilization

During cleaning, sterilization is a more complex process than disinfection. We sterilize our devices to kill microorganisms such as bacteria, spores, and fungi. Since these are hydroponic systems that are supposed to be kept indoors, we will study how to sterilize our devices with chemical cleaning agents. We can also use heat and filtration, but they are more complicated, and better suited for large-scale cultivation processes.

Unlike disinfection, we don't want to sterilize as often. For disinfection, some methods are best used daily or weekly. Sterilization must be used much less often because it is not only unnecessary but can also damage our system and our factories. First, sterilization takes longer and can leave unpleasant byproducts if you do not rinse thoroughly. In sterilization, we will mainly deal with the sterilization of our trays and tanks, as well as the interior of each tube to be cleaned.

The two most common chemical cleaners for sterilization are bleach and hydrogen peroxide. Bleach usually contains sodium hypochlorite as the active ingredient. It is the same chemical used to disinfect wastewater. Bleach is an excellent sterilizer, but it can leave marks on our devices. So if you're choosing a bleach, be prepared to rinse everything you've cleaned with two or three times. After collecting the plants, but before preparing the next batch for cultivation, it's a good time for a lightening bath.

Conclusion: You should not sterilize too often, as this can damage your plants. A good time for sterilization is the time between harvesting and preparing for a new harvest. If you use bleach for sterilization, be sure to rinse it two or three times later to prevent residue from damaging your plants.

Tank maintenance

As for our gardens, it is clear that we have a favorite section. All green is as pretty and exciting as it grows. The habit of leaf litter to remove, can be simple, because it's nice to nudge our factory and see how they are doing. Although it is easy to focus on the mountain, we cannot forget the importance of the bottom of our system. Without a nutrient reservoir, our plants would not have what they need to grow and we would only have a dead garden.

Our tanks are such an important part of our hydroponic systems that it is our duty to ensure that they are kept in perfect condition. To do this, you will have to adapt to the different stages and behaviors to ensure you keep control of the tanks.

The first step we should take is to make sure our tanks are at the right temperature. If we let our tanks get too hot, the oxygen content drops and the conditions for root rot develop. We want to keep our nutrient solution at around 65-75 degrees. If our tanks are too cold, we can always get an aquarium heater or a heating pad to increase the temperature. If our tanks are too hot, different options are available. We can get a cooler, overshadow our settings, or add a few ice cubes to our solution. We also want to make sure that after painting our tank black, we add a coat of white paint to reflect better than absorb heat.

If your hydroponic garden uses a circulation system, be sure to check the water level and fill the tank. We lose water through evaporation and the processes that our plants go through. This means that losing water is part of the gardening experience, so we must be ready to replenish the lost resources. This is especially important for small systems, since losing water in a small system is a bigger problem.

Once a week or every two weeks, you should consider changing the water in the tank. A process can be very specific to any garden. Knowing when to make a change can help you grow. However, wear it every two weeks to start. You can use the EC counter to find out when the time is right. Although the EC reader tells us the amount of fertilizer in our solutions, it does not divide us by the amount of nutrients remaining. Our plants do not consume all nutrients in the same way, some are absorbed and processed faster than others process. This means that even if we check the values with our EC meter and find that there are enough nutrients, we can actually have too much of one type and too little of another. After changing the water, we can provide our plants with a freshly balanced nutrient solution. It also gives us the ability to disinfect our tanks.

When we talk about our EC meters, we want to make sure that we perform regular EC checks. Of course, the numbers we intend to use here depend on the plants we grow. You must now check the corresponding EC values for the selected system. You also want to check your pH regularly. We know we want to keep the pH between 5.5 and 6.5.

The most important step is to have your pumps checked regularly. You want to control all the deposits in your pumps. We want to do it because nothing kills the garden faster than a broken pump. Be sure to clean the pumps and remove any buildup of nutrients. This significantly contributes to keeping the garden healthy and keeping the tank as intended.

Conclusion: Keep the tank between 65 and 75 degrees. Check the water level and top up frequently. Change the water in the tank every two weeks. Use an EC meter and a pH test to check the values. Check the pumps regularly to prevent them from clogging.

Salt build-up and salt combustion

Have you ever seen a garden with a layer of white (or off-white) crystalline crust on plant stems or on the ground? This is known as salt buildup and is very harmful to your plants. Salt buildup can cause salt burns. The burning of salt around the roots results in the death of the stem at the base of the plant. This leads to wilting in the hottest periods of the day and can even open up this area of your plant as a perfect treatment for diseases.

Salt buildup occurs when the substrate grows faster and the moisture evaporates faster than plants can consume nutrients. The humidity evaporates, but the nutrients remain and increase the EC values in the environment. The good news is that salt buildup is easy to use as long as you know what you are up to. This white crust on the stems and on top of the growing medium is dead. When you see this white crust and find that your plants have slowed down, darkened or are growing abnormally slowly, you should have all the signs you need to diagnose salt formation. One way to confirm your suspicion is to read the solution that follows from the topic. If the EC increases during draining, you are almost certain to have a salt build-up problem.

If you have found that salt has accumulated in the garden, you should rinse the surface. Although some gardeners flush their system with clean water, it can have a negative impact. If the plant is already growing, a decrease in osmotic pressure can cause the plants to absorb a ton of moisture around the roots. This can lead to broken fruit or weak, weak vegetative growth.

A healthier approach to flushing the growth medium is to use a pre-flushed rinse solution, as in any hydroponic store. You can also rinse with a nutrient solution, which is a third of its normal strength. Depending on your configuration, you may need to change this every few weeks, e.g. B. if you have a drainage and drainage system in a hot climate where it evaporates easily.

Conclusion: The accumulation of salt can be recognized by the white crust on the top of the substrate and the bottom of the stems of the plants. This is due to evaporation which leaves nutrients there. Use a risible nutrient solution with 1/3 of the regular strength to remove deposits.

Seaweed

If you run a hydroponic garden, you have to take care of the algae at some point, I promise. It is therefore important to know what to look for. Algae look like a slimy growth that adheres to different parts of your whole . It can be brown, green, reddish or black. You shouldn't be surprised if you find long chains of algae in your system, and you shouldn't be surprised if it seems to come out of nowhere. Algae can grow very quickly.

Seaweed also smells very bad. It smells musty and earthy. When a ton of algae decays in your body, it creates an unpleasant odor, which can be a sign of a serious buildup of algae on your hands.

Seaweed can be a real pain. First of all, it looks really disgusting. However, much worse than its aesthetic value and its odor, algae can easily block drops, pumps and any other element of the hydroponic system that tends to get clogged. As we have seen, it can easily kill your garden. Not only that, but if you have a serious problem with algae, it can even blocks growing substrates and steal oxygen from your plants. When this happens, it can increase the biological demand for oxygen in your system. This means that your plants do not have enough oxygen, which can strangle their roots. If the algae attach directly to the roots of the plants, they can expose the plants to the risk of pathogens such as pythium.

Algae alone can really suck, but they get worse when they start to collapse and collapse. In this case, the toxins can actually be released into your system. These toxins then serve as a food source for pathogenic fungi. When it starts, the mushrooms can suddenly come out and take a strong position in your system.

Most hydroponic growers tolerate a small number of algae in their system as it is difficult to get rid of it. If you take care of your aquarium and clean it, you can also take care of the algae at this time. Make sure to rub your systems between the bars to remove algae that enters the system. Some producers use algae products in their nutrient solutions to kill algae. However, it can also damage our plants. In addition, algae grow back quite quickly after using algaecide products. This means that soon after, you will need to add more algaecide agents to endanger the health of your plants.

Conclusion: Some algae are fine, but a serious problem must be resolved before breaking down or blocking the pumps and system components. Clean by hand instead of using seaweed.

Maintain root health

When it comes to root health, hunger, suffocation, chemical damage, pathogens, temperature or EC / pH are the most common causes of death. The main cause of root death and poor growth indicators is suffocation. Many pathogens attack a healthy root system only when damaged by bad conditions. Asphyxiation occurs when no oxygen reaches the plants, for example, when our tanks contain too much decaying organic matter, slow rivers or too many plants fighting for enough oxygen.

When the roots start to choke for lack of oxygen, the toxins start to multiply. Some plants will try to grow new roots to find other sources of oxygen, but many will get up and die. If your plants are not getting enough oxygen, add oxygen stone to the tank.

If your system does not contain enough nutrients, it affects the root system as well as the top of the plant. However, it is more difficult to say that there is a fundamental problem. The lack of phosphate makes the roots brown and you notice a decrease in the number of lateral branches. A calcium deficiency thins the root system and develops a diseased brown color. A manganese deficiency makes the root system shorter and more sensitive than usual and you notice that the tips turn brown. These are the tips you need for your nutrient solution and your tank.

Another thing that can damage the roots of our plants is an unbalanced EC and pH. An unbalanced system causes strong inhibition of the roots. At higher EC values, water is lost from the roots and leads to the death of the roots. It is a common reaction of plants with a lower EC. If the pH becomes too high or too low, it damages to the roots and create problems with nutrient absorption can be observed. However, plants are sweeter with fluctuating pH values than with EC values.

For root diseases, configurations with a nutrient circulation system present the greatest risk, as the solution cycle can easily transmit pathogens to all of our plants. Some pathogens attack the roots of the hydroponic system so that they are easier to identify, while others seem almost invisible. Whether they appear or not, all pathogens reduce the growth of your plants and the amount they give. The most common pathogens that spoil our roots are Didymella, Verticillium, Olpidium, Plasmopara, Pythium, Fusarium and Phytophthora.

Pathogens that affect your roots can come from a variety of sources. They can float in the air; occur in water, in the nutrient medium, they come from insects and pests, infected plant substances and even seeds and dust. Airborne pathogens that damage your roots are rare, but can still occur. Soil is one of the most common sources of infection. Soil can enter the hydroponic system through hands, shoes, dust in the air, through our equipment and even through the water we use in our tank.

Root diseases and the pathogens that cause them like to attack plants that are already under high stress. Since stressed plants leave the system open to attack, the best way to defend yourself against these pathogens is to make sure the plants are healthy and not exposed to excessive stress, for example if the stems are pruned too often. Another reason for stress is that our roots are not getting enough oxygen, for example, when algae has become a serious problem.

One of the best behaviors we can adopt is to make sure we take the time to check the root system of our plants. Most of us want to bury at the top, where everything is green and beautiful. While it is important that we take care of our blouses, we cannot forget the stockings. Checking the roots regularly is a great tool to grasp the problem before it becomes a crisis. If the plant looks wilted or discolored, check the root system.

If you find that the plant has or may have root diseases, you should first remove it from the garden and destroy it. If the plant is sick and you leave it in the system, there is a risk of this disease spreading to other healthy plants. These pathogens can survive and move from one culture to another. It is therefore important to disinfect and sterilize the hydroponic system between crops.

Conclusion: Root health is just as important as the health of our sweatshirts. Lack of oxygen is the most common problem for our roots. Avoid stress in plants by regularly checking the EC and pH values. Identify root problems so that you can get rid of diseased plants before transferring them to healthy plants.

Fruit and Flowering

Regarding the problems of fruiting and flowering of our plants, there can be many different reasons. These range from a lack of fruit development to physiological disorders such as end-of-flower rot. Your fruit may have skin problems such as blemishes, streaks, silvering or uneven color. Another problem is the division of the fruit, which leads to awful-looking plants that are terribly distorted.

Many hydroponic crops begin to flower and bear fruit when they reach the right age. If there is a problem with fruiting, you may have problems dropping flowers. Then the flowers and fruit fall from the plant before they are finished. It can be caused by external problems, but it can also be internal, for example when our plants are under excessive stress. If the air temperature is too high, many plants will fall on the flowers. The point at which heat affects plants is different for each type. If your plants don't have enough light, the flowers can also fall. Lack of light can also inhibit the growth of the whole plant.

A drop of flowerscan also be caused by a lack of nutrients. The most common causes of falling flowers due to deficiency occur when our plants do not receive enough nitrogen or phosphorus from the nutrient solution we produce. Water stress can also cause flowers to fall. It is the stress caused by a bad irrigation system or too high EC. For this reason, we want to make sure that we regularly check the EC values of our nutrients.

Another reason for falling fruit is that the fruit is too heavy for the plant to hold. This may be due to the weight of the fruit or the weight of the vegetative growth itself. For this reason, we want to make sure that we prune our plants in a healthy way that encourages manageable growth, e.g. B. when we crown our plants. If larger fruits grow on our plants, it can lead to the fall of small fruits. This can actually help the growth of larger, healthier fruits. We can also consider removing the berries so that the energy necessary for their growth is diverted.

Conclusion: Flowering and fruit problems are generally associated with stress. Take care of your plants, remove unhealthy fruits and support heavy plants to prevent them from falling.

CHAPTER 6

PEST CONTROL

We created our own hydroponic garden, collected plants, discovered the nutrients and wondered how we could take care of them. But now we have a completely new problem: pests. Our configuration provided the perfect environment for the growth of our plants. But it also created an environment that loves parasites, and we even filled them with tons of healthy plants for them to eat. It would be nice if they offered a service to our plants, but all they want is to eat them and leave them withered and yellowed.

In this chapter, we will look at the most common pests that hydroponics are exposed to and how to spot them in your own garden. Our best defense against pests is to prevent them from planting our home gardens. Therefore, we learn some of the techniques with which they can be recognized early and prevent infestation.

Pests are not the only problem we face as hydroponic breeders. Illness is also something we need to be alert to when we recognize it, identify it and manage it. To this end, we will examine some of the most common diseases and how to prevent them. Much of this information is covered in Chapter 5, so we will often refer to it here.

Common hydroponic pests

Although there are many pests that can try to make our gardens home, some are more common than others. These pests fall into five key categories: mites, thrips, fungal mosquitoes, whiteflies and aphids. If you are in a pest, you can expect it to fall into one of these five categories.

Spinning

Of the five types of mites, it is particularly annoying. Although these little guys are less than a millimeter long, they are really little spiders. Because they are so small, they tend to damage plants before noticing that they have taken care of your garden. The damage caused by spider mites looks like small brown and yellow spots on the leaves of your plants. Although they don't look serious, with only a few bites, the damage quickly adds to the real chaos in your garden.

To identify the invasion of spider mites, two key signs should be noted. While damage to your plants may be an important sign, it doesn't specifically say that the problem is with mites. To detect the invasion of spider mites, you should check the plants to see if you can see a spider web like a spider . Another way to check for mites is to gently wipe the bottom of the leaves with a tissue or clean cloth. If you leave with blood strips, you will be informed that you have a mite problem.

One way to control mites is to wash the plants with a powerful hose or spray bottle. The power of water can often knock down plant mites and drown them in the ground. Spiders also have natural predators, from ladybugs to varnishes, and you might consider adding these beneficial insects to your garden to feed the spider population.

Aphids

These little people are also known as plant lice. And like lice, they are not so funny. These tiny, soft-bodied pests can position themselves in any environment. They reproduce faster than rabbits, so you must manage the aphid invasion as soon as possible. These pests generally measure a quarter of an inch and can appear in green, yellow, pink, black or gray varieties.

Aphids like to eat plant juices and can be chewed on stems, leaves, buds, fruit or roots. They are particularly interested in the latter parts of the system. If your leaves turn out to be deformed or yellowed, a drop test can reveal aphids. They also leave behind a sticky substance called honeydew. This sweet substance can attract other types of pests, which is why aphids are particularly annoying little creatures. This substance can also cause the growth of fungi such as soot, which can make branches or leaves uncomfortably black. The aphids can also transmit the virus from one plant to another, allowing unpleasant pathogens to spread more quickly.

As with spider mites, spraying water on the leaves can remove them and make it difficult for them to get to your plants. If the infestation is significant, vacuuming the plants with flour can limit them and convince them that it is time to continue. Wiping plants with a mixture of soap and water can also help kill and germinate them.

Thrips

Like spiders and aphids, these little guys are small. Often they are only about 5 millimeters. It's hard to see these little boys, but they leave the damage as clear as daylight. If you see tiny metallic black spots on the leaves, you probably have thrips in a garden. The leaves that attack Thrips often turn brown and become very dry because Thrips like to suck their juice.

Thrips are small and have a black or straw color. They have a slim body and two pairs of wings. Because they are so small, they look like black threads to the naked eye. They like to eat in large groups and fly away when they disturb them. They push the eggs into the flowers and leaves, and the hatching takes only a few days to give the impression that the invasion of thrips has occurred unexpectedly.

Since thrips like to lay eggs in plants, it is very important to remove dead or fallen plant material. If you followed the last chapter, you know you should do it anyway, as this helps to avoid many of the problems that can affect our hydroponic gardens. Make sure to examine the plants for damage from the thrip and remove any infected ones. Weaning the plants will also help reduce their populations. Ladybugs, laces and small pirate insects feed on thrips and can benefit your garden.

Fungal decay

Mushroom mosquitoes are strange. Adult mushroom mosquitoes are not interested in destroying the garden. But their larvae like to chew the roots of plants, which slows growth and opens the plant to infection. In extreme cases, fungal mosquito larvae can actually kill plants. They like very humid and very humid areas. You will likely notice adult fungal mosquitoes before a problem occurs. In adulthood, mosquitoes are about three millimeters long and look like mosquitoes. They are usually gray-black in color with two long legs and clean wings. Their larvae have shiny black heads with a whitish transparent body.

Adults generally live for a week and lay up to 300 eggs during this period. The larvae take half a week, but when they do, they start a two-week diet, the main dish being the roots of your plants. When they feed on your plants, they cause wilting, inhibit their growth and cause the leaves to turn yellow. These evil little things can have multiple generations living on the same plant.

If you suspect a fungal infection with mosquitoes, check the plants by gently turning the soil around their stems and looking for larvae. If you examine the plant and suddenly release a group of adult mosquitoes, you need to get rid of this plant. They really like wet soils, so don't water your plants. If you have a problem with fungal mosquitoes, prolonged drainage of the potting soil will help kill the larvae and affect the development of fungal mosquito eggs. You can also spray the plants with a combination of peppermint, cinnamon and sesame oil. This mixture is called a flying insecticide and helps get rid of mosquitoes.

White flies

Ants, about as large ß are like spider mites, look like little white ß Moths inhabit plants. They are easier to spot, but because they fly away when you stop, they can be difficult to kill. Like aphids, they like to suck the juices from your plant, and you see their damage as white patches and yellowing of the leaves.

They generally lay 200 to 400 eggs in clusters at the bottom of the upper leaves. These eggs hatch in about a week, leaving unattractive little nymphs that crawl on your leaves before their wings develop. These robots move away from the egg and find a place to chew the leaves. They will stay here next week before they become young adults rehearsing the garden party.

Ladybugs and lacewings like to eat whiteflies. So if you put them in the garden, you can kill the whitefly population. Weaning plants with a strong push of water also help to reduce their number. There are many organic pesticides on the market that can treat whiteflies. These pesticides can also affect other pests, but pesticides should be the last option to avoid overloading the plants.

Pest control

Now that we have an idea of the most common pests in hydroponic gardens, we are focusing on how to prevent them from entering our gardens. Many of these techniques help us identify possible infections when we try to get started. They therefore offer us early warnings to prepare us for pest control. If we continue our preventive measures and keep our eyes open for pests, we can save our plants from a lot of damage and we ourselves have a lot of time to bring the problem to the fore.

When it comes to pests, it's also important to understand that not all pests are the same. This does not only mean that whiteflies are different from fungal mosquitoes. This means that the mushroom mosquito on the west coast is different from the mushroom mosquito on the east coast. Not all prevention or destruction solutions work. A particular pesticide can be used to kill mosquitoes in the east, but those in the west may have become resistant to them. For this reason, it is important to check with your local hydroponics store to see if region-specific information is needed to resolve the pest problem.

One way to prevent pests is to limit their ability to enter our garden. We can do this in different ways. Mosquito nets protect against parasites. We also want to limit traffic in and around our configurations. If possible, our configurations provide significant advantages if they can be protected by airlock entrances, as they offer the safest protection against pests and pathogens. The locks can be doubled to create a space in front of the garden where you can wipe off dirt and insects or eggs that allow your clothes to travel freely.

Use sticky traps around your plants to determine if there are pests in your garden. The yellow and blue sticky traps are useful because they attract different pests. So you need to make sure that you are using both types to get the best results. Place traps near garden entrances such as doors or ventilation systems. Also be sure to place one or two near the plant stems to catch pests that prefer snacks on the bottom pieces, such as aphids or fungal mosquitoes. Make it a habit to check these traps regularly as they can give you a good idea of life in your garden.

Traps help us fight infections, but they are not a reliable method of preventing pests. Traps should be used with personal on-site inspections. This means that you need to check the pest plants several times a week. Take a clean cloth and check the bottom of the sheets. Check the roots of the mosquito larvae. You can visually inspect the top of the leaves. Look for signs of yellowing or stinging, as described above.

Be sure to eliminate weeds that take root in your garden, as these plants only absorb resources from your garden and provide food for pests. Of course, also remove dead or fallen plant substances. This includes leaves, but also fallen fruit, buds and petals.

Before introducing new plants to your garden, be sure to quarantine them so you can examine them for pests. If necessary, you can use a magnifying glass. Carefully check new plants by checking all parts of the plants and potting soil before moving them.

By creating a plant inspection system and schedule, you can prevent the entry of pests that damage the garden or cause a lot of headaches. A watchful eye gives you an advantage in preventing and treating pest problems of all kinds. Remember that a strong defense is the best crime when it comes to keeping plants healthy and harmless.

Typical hydroponic diseases

The disease is terrible, whether it be humans or our plants. In the last chapter, we saw how we maintain a healthy garden to keep pathogens from staying in our systems. In this article, we will look at the most common diseases that growers in hydroponics are exposed to.

Iron deficiency

If your plants don't get enough iron, they can't produce enough chlorophyll. This means that their leaves turn light yellow with strong green veins. Untreated leaves glow white and then die. This will stop the growth and death of the whole plant. These iron deficiency symptoms are similar to some other illnesses, so it is important to confirm an iron deficiency before starting treatment.

To diagnose iron deficiency, you need to test your growing surgery. Do a pH test and check the numbers. A value greater than 7.0 can prevent many plants from absorbing iron. Also take an EC measurement and check your values. You may have an imbalance. Remember that the EC control does not confirm the amount of each nutrient in your solution. You can therefore consider changing the nutrient solution to a freshly balanced batch.

If you have found an iron deficiency, you should first adjust the pH and EC value and put everything in the correct range. You can also buy liquid iron to spray the plants. Spray liquid iron directly on the leaves. Liquid iron is just a quick fix, not a solution. So if it works, you need to improve the nutrient solution so that it contains more iron.

Powdery Mildew

Powdery mildew is an easily recognizable fungal disease. Due to the type of fungus, this disease develops in plants in areas with less moisture in the growing medium and loves it especially when the humidity on the surface of the plants is high. This mold begins on the young leaves of the plants and looks like small bubbles on them. These bubbles are slightly raised and cause the leaves to curl. This fold shows the lower parts of the leaf structure for easier access. The infected leaves appear to be covered with an unsightly white powder. Untreated leaves turn brown and fall off. It mainly affects new leaves, which is why the leaves of older and more mature plants are generally free from infections.

To deal with mold, you want to cut off part of the plant to open it for better air circulation. This helps to reduce the humidity of the plant so that powdery mildew is less favored. Remove any leaves that have already been infected and clean up any fallen plants. A spray of 60% water and 40% milk can be used every two weeks to prevent the buildup of powdery mildew. Also wash your plants from time to time, as this prevents mildew and various pests. A fungicide can be used when the problem is extreme, but it can also harm plants.

Gray mold

Gray mold has different names, such as ghost ash or ghost spot. Whatever name you name, you can easily find it. It starts with small gray spots on your plants that turn into a fuzzy gray abrasion that absorbs your plant until it turns completely brown and is nothing more than a disgusting porridge. Gray mold can be found on a number of plants, but it is particularly known to anyone who has grown strawberries because it completely destroys infected berries.

Gray mold likes to settle on the bottom of the plant and in areas where the plant provides the most shade. Usually it starts with wilted flowers and then spreads quickly to the leaves and stem. He really likes these very humid areas. Infected plants start to rot and untreated gray mold is one of the most repulsive diseases to fight. Spores such as low temperatures and high humidity can penetrate directly into healthy plant tissue, making plants particularly susceptible to cutting.

Pruning plants or adding a grid improves air circulation and reduces plant humidity, making gray mold less desirable. You can also use a small fan to increase the air flow around your plants. Always remove any fallen plant material. If you spray the plants in the morning, let them dry so that gray mold is less interested in thc bcd. Fungicides can also help fight infections with gray mold.

Disease prevention

In the last chapter, we saw how we take care of our hydroponic gardens. These steps are also important because they help us prevent disease in our gardens. Since they are directly related to our conversation here in this chapter, you will learn a lot from this information. However, this is crucial in preventing diseases in the garden, so you need to reassure them.

The most important thing we can do to help our plants not get sick is to make sure they are healthy and not too stressed. This means that we want to check our pH and EC values regularly to make sure they are within the correct range. We also want to make sure that we clean our tank from time to time and that we have a schedule for removing the old solution and filling it with a new, freshly balanced solution. This helps your plants stay healthy and keep pathogens away.

You also want to keep your garden as clean as possible. As with pests, you can wipe and clean with a two-door airlock system before entering the garden. This way you can remove the dirt from your person. It is the most effective way to introduce pathogens into your system. Remember to wash your hands and all the tools you want to use in the garden before you start playing. Clean your shoes and take off the jacket or outerwear you wear.

Dispose of spilled substances as soon as they appear to prevent additional moisture and moisture from entering the plants when they attract disease. Also be sure to remove dead plant material as soon as you see it. Dead plants become breeding grounds for pests and diseases. Check your plants regularly for disease and remove any signs of serious infection. Wash your plants twice a week to avoid pests or infections that could get caught.

By being vigilant and taking care of your garden, you can prevent the spread of disease and make sure you grow beautiful, healthy plants.

CHAPTER 7

AVOID MYTHS AND ERRORS

Our time together is almost over. Before going into your garden, let's take a look at some of the mistakes and myths that are common in discussions about hydroponics. By treading myths to find the truth and learn from the mistakes of those who have come to us, we can use the knowledge and avoid making the same mistakes.

Error: Parameters Difficult to Use

When setting up a hydroponic garden, you must take into account the difficulty of its use. Do you have trouble accessing the plants in the background because you put a garden on the wall? Are you going to get into the light every time you try to hold the bed because the space is too small and narrow?

When planning your garden, it is important to take into account elements such as the physical space it will occupy. You want to be sure that you can easily reach all of the plants. If you roll on the lights or throw your back to reach the plants, the configuration is not very good. You may at some point spoil or neglect something. Think about how you navigate the garden. Make sure you can achieve anything.

You also want to make sure that you can easily enter the tank. Think about how it can cause problems when it comes to changing the nutrient solution. Do you have room for a grow tray while you are playing with the tank? If not, how did you do it?

In Chapter 5, we saw all the different steps we take to maintain our hydroponic garden. Reread these steps before installing the garden and make sure that you can use the configuration to enter the garden and perform these actions. Otherwise, you should rethink your project.

Myth: hydroponic gardens are only for illegal substances

It seems that whenever there is information on hydroponics, it is linked to an illegal harvest stopped by the police. This has created a stigma on hydroponics that he doesn't really deserve. This is not because many illegal growers use hydroponics setups that hydroponics is only used for illegal purposes.

As we saw above, we went through the whole book on hydroponics and didn't mention any drugs. We looked at how hydroponics will help our herb gardens produce 30% more aromatic oils. We talked about vegetables and fruits. We never talked about illegal substances.

Mistake: Choosing the wrong crop for your climate

You hear about a new crop in one of the gardens you view online. It seems like growing can be fun, a berry you've never heard of before, and people say it works great in a hydroponic configuration. You order seeds, plant them and multiply them, but that does not produce the desired results. To see what didn't work, search the Google system a bit and find that it must be in a very hot and dry environment. And you are living the coldest winter of your life.

Different plants want different climates and nothing will be more disappointing than trying to grow a plant that just doesn't like the climate you can offer. We must always look for the plants we want to grow. We can easily do this via Google or in our local hydroponic store to speak to employees.

Myth: Hydroponics must be done indoors

In this book, we have talked a lot about indoor hydroponics. This decision highlighted the fact that we can grow indoor hydroponics. There are many people who do not have access to outside property where they can plant a garden. Most people who live in a residential building have at most one balcony, and many do not even have many. Thanks to the fact that you can have an indoor garden, hydroponics gives more people to the garden.

But that doesn't mean you can't have an outdoor hydroponic garden. When we grow our indoor gardens, we can control the seasons and play an active role in maintaining humidity and temperature, as long as the rising lights are on, and more. If we grow outdoors, we can save money if we let the light grow with the sun, but we also open our garden to a higher risk of pests and diseases. However, hydroponics can be done anywhere.

Error: Incorrect system selection for configuration

You can also call it "no test". Just like choosing plants that suit your climate, you also need to make sure that you choose plants that work well in your setup. Some plants work better on different systems. Some people want less water; Some want slower drainage, others want more water, and others want faster drainage.

It is important to study the plants you want to put in your garden. There are hundreds of websites with information about each plant you want to grow. They tell you about the plant's pH and EC value, how much they love their environment, how much water they want, and what type of hydroponic configuration is best for them. We've looked at a handful of them throughout the book, but there's no way to cover them all. But Google is your friend.

So be sure to research and plan your garden. Preparing with information avoids costly mistakes. Not only does growth cost, it also takes time and you waste weeks before realizing that growing this plant is a losing battle.

Myth: Hydroponics is very expensive

If you go to the hydroponic store, see all the prices, and buy more than what you really need, it will be expensive. However, the number of hobbies depends on the severity you want to take on and you can always start slowly.

There are many ways to cut costs early in the garden. If you search online, you will find hundreds of independent guides after you start setting up hydroponics.

Error: scaling operation too early

Going overweight can be a terrible mistake. First of all, it means investing a lot of money in growth right outside the door. Before doing this, you must have at least some experience in hydroponics. Another big problem is that until you gain experience, you don't know how to take care of your garden and that each phase of the operational cycle will be an educational experience.

Myth: Hydroponics is not natural

What happened to the plant that was sunk into the ground and made it grow? Hydroponics seems to require a lot of work to do the same. The plants also appear larger. It seems that something unnatural is happening here. These must be all the chemicals used in the solution.

Of course, this myth is just plain stupid. We grow plants and use a natural mixture in our bowls. We combine the nutrients with each other, but these are all natural nutrients that plants absorb anyway. Hydroponics is just a growing system. We grow healthy plants like any gardener. No coarse chemicals are used for better growth than the soil. All we do is take advantage of the plant's natural desires to give it the most pleasant growing experience.

Error: No maintenance of the garden

I know I know. You have heard it before. But this is the number one mistake that new breeders make, so we'll talk about it for the last time. The point is, taking care of a garden does not just mean changing the water. It does not only mean that we are looking at the garden when the plants look sick and infected and get to work. Taking care of our gardens is a commitment that every gardener must respect.

Did you spill something? Better to wipe it off. Do you have a dead plant in the bin or on the ground around your set? It is best to clean it and get rid of it. Infestation and infections like to develop under these conditions. So check your plants, test the water, clean the beds and show them some love. You do not let your dog sleep in your own trash. So why should you leave your plants? Maintaining the garden is the most important thing you can do as a new breeder.

Treat your plants well.

Mistake: forgetting the pleasure

If you are growing because you want to sell your crop, there is good reason to do so. But try to have fun. For many, a pleasant pastime gives them plenty of rest. If you start making money, you can easily lose sight of it. Remember to take the time to smell the roses or tomatoes, whatever you grow.

LAST WORDS

We have come a long way in this book. Starting with the definition of hydroponics, we have discussed a lot of information to help you get started in your own hydroponic garden. Before closing, let's take a quick look at what we discussed and share the words where to go.

Hydroponics has been around for centuries, but it is only just starting to generate keen interest. Setting up and maintaining these gardens may require some work, but it's a great way to grow plants. We have focused here on those who wish to get started in hydroponics and have therefore adapted our information to beginners. However, the lessons we have discussed have everything a beginner needs to get started and go to an expert.

We have six basic parameters from which to choose with regard to the type of system we want to configure. We have seen how to set up deep water, humidity management and drip systems. These are the simplest systems for self-configuration and for beginners, but there are also aeroponics, drainage and flow systems as well as nutrient film techniques. These systems are more complex than those recommended for beginners, but I recommend that you study them more if you are more comfortable with hydroponics.

We consider four key elements as a cycle of hydroponic gardening activities. These are dirt, sowing, lighting and cutting. If we understand how each of these works, we can manage the growth cycle of our plants. There are many dirt options and various lighting options available. Finding the right combination requires research, but in the end, you have to decide which plants you want to grow.

Speaking of plants, we have seen that there are many plants that work very well in hydroponic gardens. Herbs grown in a hydroponic garden contain 30% more aromatic oils than herbs grown in the soil. Lettuce particularly likes hydroponics. Each plant has its own preferences regarding the amount of water, the pH it prefers and the temperature it needs to grow. For this reason, we need to examine our plants and make sure that we only grow those that are compatible with each other.

We have also learned to mix our own nutritional solutions to give our plants what they need to thrive. There are also many ready-to-buy options. Taking control of our own mix is another way to get closer to our plants and give them our best. We have looked at some of the most common pests that infect our plants. However, we have not addressed them all. It will take the whole book. The pests we have fought are most likely treated, but that does not mean that they are the only ones. It is good that we have also learned how to prevent pests. Preventive measures are the term, which prevented us from doing also help us to detect pests that we have not, fought. If you find something in one of your traps that you don't recognize, you know it's time to investigate further. Also keep in mind that not all insects are pests. Some help us by eating parasites!

Infection is a threat to all gardens. Our most important tool to keep our plants from attacking harmful pathogens is to make sure our plants are beautiful and resilient. We clean our gardens, provide them with nutrients tailored to their preferences, give them the love and care they need, and take care of their health and stress.

Finally, we looked at the typical mistakes of budding hydroponic gardeners. We also blew up hydroponic myths to dispel the lies and lies surrounding our newly discovered hobby. If you are looking for advice or mistakes online, you will see many discussions with hydroponic gardeners that have been specially written to give beginners like you the easiest and most enjoyable time to get into this form of gardening.

If you are enthusiastic, we recommend that you start planning your garden now. You have to give it a seat and choose the system that is most attractive to you and your skills. Register the plants you want to grow the most and collect information about them. Which environment do you prefer? What temperature How much light do you need? What pH value?

Once you know which plants, you want to grow and which system you want, you can start creating a shopping list. In addition to the system configuration devices, do not forget the pH test kits and the EC meter. Also make sure you have cleaning supplies, as you already know the importance of decontaminating and sterilizing your equipment. It is also a good time to make a maintenance schedule.

After receiving this information, you can return to this book and use it as a guide to go through each step of the growth process. The information we have discussed will take you from a beginner and turn you into a pro with the use of practice. Above all, don't forget to have fun!

CPSIA information can be obtained
at www.ICGtesting.com
Printed in the USA
BVHW010857300421
605946BV00015B/731